So Much Secret Labor

So Much

Secret Labor

JAMES WRIGHT AND TRANSLATION

Anne Wright, Saundra Rose Maley, and Jeffrey Katz

Wesleyan University Press
Middletown, Connecticut

Wesleyan University Press
Middletown CT 06459
www.wesleyan.edu/wespress

Manufactured in the United States of America
Designed and composed in Adobe Caslon Pro, American
Typewriter, Aurelly Signature, and Avenir types by
Chris Crochetière, BW&A Books, Inc.

Library of Congress Cataloging-in-Publication Data
Names: Wright, Anne (Edith Anne), author. | Maley, Saundra, author. |
Katz, Jeffrey (Librarian), author.
Title: So much secret labor : James Wright and translation / Anne Wright,
Saundra Rose Maley, Jeffrey Katz.
Description: Middletown, Connecticut : Wesleyan University Press, [2025] |
Includes bibliographical references and index. | Summary: "A collection that
weaves together literary criticism, translation studies, and biography to explore
how the art of poetic translation impacted the original poetry of James Wright,
including facsimiles of archival material such as notebook pages of Wright's
translations in progress, with manuscript notes by Wright and Robert Bly"—
Provided by publisher.

Identifiers: LCCN 2024031470 (print) | LCCN 2024031471 (ebook) |
ISBN 780819501578 (cloth) | ISBN 9780819501585 (paperback) |
ISBN 9780819501592 (ebook)
Subjects: LCSH: Wright, James, 1927-1980—Criticism and interpretation. |
Poetry, Modern—20th century—Translations into English—History and criti-
cism. | Translating and interpreting—United States—History—20th century.
Classification: LCC PS3573.R5358 Z95 2025 (print) | LCC PS3573.R5358 (ebook) |
DDC 811/.54—dc23/eng2022024118
LC record available at https://lccn.loc.gov/2024031470
LC ebook record available at https://lccn.loc.gov/2024031471

cloth   978-0-8195-0157-8
paper   978-0-8195-0158-5
ebook   978-0-8195-0159-2

5 4 3 2 1

Publication of this book is funded by the
Beatrice Fox Auerbach Foundation Fund
at the Hartford Foundation for Public Giving

Contents

Preface

James Wright and Translations

ANNE WRIGHT

THIS IS NOT A CONVENTIONAL BOOK of poetry in translation. Readers will not find just a selection of translations by poet James Wright (1927–1980). Saundra Maley and I thought long and hard about how to shape the book and, after many attempted starts, we finally decided to make it a demonstration of the evolution of Wright's interest in the art of translation, and of how that affected his own poetry.

After working together for seven years on *A Wild Perfection*, a collection of James's letters, we took some much-needed time off before embarking on a new project. This present book is the result of a request from Suzanna Tamminen, editor-in-chief of Wesleyan University Press, to assemble something concerning James's translation of German and Spanish poets. We were happy to accept this idea!

Although our work was slow, we never gave up on the book. On and off we kindled our energy and met in Washington DC and Rhode Island for rewarding work sessions. Then, in 2018, we invited Jeffrey Katz, the former director of libraries at Bard College, to become our third editor. His agreement was most fortuitous. Encouraged by his energy, scholarship, enthusiasm, and willingness to visit the James Wright collection at the University of Minnesota's Elmer L. Andersen Library in Minneapolis, as Saundra and I had done previously, we worked together to finish our book.

Now, much later, after many long, long phone calls and copious correspondence, we have completed *So Much Secret Labor*.

SAUNDRA MALEY, JEFF KATZ, AND I believe that when James Wright worked on translations he was trying to get to the roots, the very essence, of poetry. He felt that in the 1950s and '60s most American poets were provincial in their ideas about the poetry of other countries and in other languages, so he set out on various and extensive adventures in translation work. He found the work of poets in other languages a vital help for his own poetry.

James Wright was born on December 13, 1927, in Martins Ferry, Ohio. His parents, Jessie and Dudley Wright, left school to be of financial help to their respective families when they were fourteen years old. During the Great Depression Dudley never lost his job at the Hazel Atlas Glass Factory but the family remained far from affluent. James remembered putting cardboard in his shoes when the soles wore out, but he and his family never went hungry.

When James was a student at the Shreve High School in Martins Ferry, Ohio, he did his first translations from the Latin of Catullus. He was encouraged and inspired by Helen McNeely Sheriff, his Latin instructor, and Elizabeth Willerton, his English teacher. Both teachers recognized him as a gifted young man and encouraged him to develop his full potential as a scholar.

After graduation from high school, James did a stint in Japan with the peace time army, where he became acquainted with Japanese poetry, a form he loved. He returned to Martins Ferry after his time in the army and was accepted at Kenyon College in Gambier, Ohio, a decision made possible by the GI Bill. I believe that, after what may have been the confining limitations of life in Martins Ferry, the bucolic setting of Gambier combined with the highly stimulating and intellectual atmosphere of the faculty must had seemed like Paradise.

He had studied Spanish at Martins Ferry High School for two years and French at Kenyon, but his serious studies in German were of utmost importance. He worked first under Professor Frederic Eberle, known as "Cap" Eberle, and, later, with Andre Hanfman. He became sufficiently proficient in German to turn to the poetry of Rilke, Goethe, Storm, and Hölderlin, among others, for his early translation work. He also thrived under the guidance of supportive members of the English Department which, in those days, included such brilliant men as John Crowe Ransom, Philip Timberlake, Andre Hanfman, and Philip Rice.

He graduated in February of 1952 and married Liberty Kardules, also from Martins Ferry. James had won a Fulbright scholarship to the University of Vienna for that fall, and, fully confident of his ability in German, he set out with Liberty to Austria. He took classes from the fall of 1952 until the spring of 1953. When the term ended he, Liberty, and baby Franz, born in Vienna that spring on March 18, traveled a bit, including a visit to England so James could view Thomas Hardy's territory, before returning to the United States.

In a letter to Robert Bly, written on July 22, 1958, he described an amazing incident that had occurred during his time in Austria:

> . . . I blundered into a classroom at Vienna where a little Italian scholar named Susini was softly lecturing. The audience consisted of five very small and withered old men—anyone else would have taken them for hoboes in America, but everybody is a hobo in Austria—and myself. And every afternoon at 3 o'clock, I think it was four days a week, I walked through that terrible cold and unheated winter city to hear Susini whisper in his beautiful, gentle, liquid voice the poems of an Austrian of whom I had never even heard.[1]

The poet was Georg Trakl.

He went on to mention that the first time he heard Susini read Trakl's "Verfall," in the company of his good friend and fellow Fulbright scholar Herbert Lindenberger, "It was as though the sea had entered the class room at the last moment, for this poem was not like any poem I had ever recognized."

James, Liberty, and their son Franz left Austria that fall of 1953 for Seattle, where James did graduate work at the University of Washington. He was a student of Theodore Roethke, Stanley Kunitz, and Wayne Burns, as well as a friend of fellow poets Carolyn Kizer, Richard Hugo, and David Wagoner. I imagine it was a smooth transition as the buildings and intellectual climate bore some resemblance to

Vienna. The campus, particularly in the spring when the cherry trees were in blossom, was outstanding. It was a stimulating and heady time. James had won the respect and admiration of friends and faculty for his capacity as a scholar and poet. Also during that time, in 1956 his first book of poetry, *The Green Wall*, won the Yale Series of Younger Poets prize and was published by Yale University Press in 1957.

In the fall of 1957 the Wright family moved again, this time to Minneapolis where James had accepted a position in the English Department at the University of Minnesota. He returned to Seattle briefly in 1959 when he defended his dissertation, *The Comic Imagination of the Young Dickens*, and received a PhD.

Despite an attractive campus, cultural advantages, and the outskirts of Minneapolis, studded with green parks and lakes, James was bitterly disappointed. He had hoped to remain in Seattle, a place he learned to love, but his plans were dashed when he found it was against the policy at that time to have recent graduates serve as faculty members.

In Minneapolis he shared an office at the University with Allen Tate. Tate, a highly praised poet and scholar, was much revered by the English Department. James, in contrast, was just a lowly assistant professor, despite the publication of *The Green Wall*. He felt overwhelmed by the responsibilities as teacher and department member, combined with work needed to finish his PhD thesis—not to mention his own writing, about which he had become discouraged. In addition, it was difficult to find a crumb of time to spend with his family that now included a new son, Marshall John, born on July 30, 1958. He was overworked, overwhelmed, and depressed by his life and the atmosphere of Minneapolis which, to him, resembled the middle west of his childhood that he had tried to escape.

Then, on July 22, 1958, about a year after he and his family had left Seattle for Minneapolis, he found a copy of a new journal, *The Fifties*, in his mailbox at the university. He proceeded to read the entire journal right then and there. Printed on the inside cover was this comment: "The editors of this magazine think that most of the poetry published in America today is too old-fashioned."[2] The contents of the magazine served as a force that changed James's outlook on poetry, his own work, and, in many ways, his life.

The Fifties, co-edited by Robert Bly and William Duffy, was a brand-new publication with brand-new ideas about poetry. On that same day James wrote the editor, Robert Bly, a long eight-page letter followed by another one the next day. Thus began what would become a long and extensive correspondence between the two poets. They met soon after the first exchange of letters and established an affectionate and complex friendship that lasted until James's death in 1980. What began as a shared love for the poetry of Georg Trakl extended into the general world of poetry and, in particular, a group of poets who wrote in Spanish.

By 1959 his life seemed to be going in two different directions. On one hand, classes at the university, his own poetic work, the troubled erosion of his marriage, as well as emotional problems and alcoholism all seemed to lead him toward serious trouble. In contrast were the heady experiences of an expansive correspondence with Bly, a deepening friendship with Bly and his wife Carol, frequent visits to their farm, and a new deep interest and engrossment in Spanish translations. I believe it was the work of translation that helped him simplify his own poems, in conjunction with the encouraging acceptance of the Blys, many long talks with Carol, as well as Robert, and many visiting poets. It was this time of tranquility away from the problems of his life that was instrumental in the change in James's poetry.

In 1962 he was divorced, and Liberty moved to San Francisco with their sons. In 1963 he was denied tenure at the University of Minnesota. However, a number of positive events came into juxtaposition at this painful and troubled time. He was offered a position as a guest professor at Macalester College in 1963, and his third book, *The Branch Will Not Break*, was published in 1963. In addition, under the editorship of E. L. Doctorow, his good friend from Kenyon College days, he translated from German a volume of the fiction of Theodor Storm entitled *The Rider on the White Horse*, published in 1964.

One of the few instances when James talked to me of his translation work was to tell me of the pleasure he had working on the Storm stories. He had worked daily at the quiet apartment of a friend and claimed the project "came at the right time."

A Guggenheim Fellowship grant made it possible for James to leave Minnesota in June of 1965 and afford to live for a year without a teaching job. He spent that summer in three places: the Bly farm, his parents' home in Ohio, and Palo Alto, California, where he stayed with his former high school English teacher, Elizabeth Willerton, now Esterly, and her husband Henry.

Then Roger Hecht, his close friend from Kenyon, persuaded him to come to New York City and try his luck. Once settled in New York at the Hotel Regent on Broadway and 104th Street he continued to work on a new manuscript, *Shall We Gather at the River*. He also applied for teaching positions in the area and was accepted by Hunter College.

James started teaching at the uptown campus of Hunter in the Bronx in the fall of 1966. We had met that spring and were married a year and day later. James left the Regent for my railroad apartment, bringing a small suitcase of clothes and a huge suitcase of books and papers. The new manuscript and many drafts of translations were among the papers. I was to learn far more about the work of all those translations when we spent our honeymoon at the Bly farm and were presented, by Robert, with copies of the books they had worked on together, published by Odin House.

For most of our marriage I knew very little about James's work as a translator. In fact he often referred to himself as a teacher first and foremost, and then a poet, but rarely mentioned working as a translator. I became familiar, through his many stories about time spent on the Bly farm, his friendship with Robert and Carol, *The Fifties*, Odin House press, and the gathering of poets on the farm. And, of course, I listened to him talk of the poets who wrote in Spanish, most of whom were new to me, but not about the actual labor of translation. I'm not even sure if he was working on any translations at that time as his attention was focused on *Shall We Gather at the River*.

Not until 1969, when Farrar, Straus and Giroux commissioned James to translate poems by Herman Hesse, was I able to see him at this work. He kept in close touch with his editor, Michael di Capua, as well as the German-speaking expert from the publishing house. The book, *Poems*, was published in 1970, followed by *Wandering* in collaboration with his son Franz. This lovely volume of prose, poetry, and drawings by Hesse came out in 1972.

1972 was an important year for James. The Poetry Center at the 92nd Street Y held an evening for Pablo Neruda, who read his poems in Spanish. James and Robert Bly were among the writers who read some of their translations of Neruda's work. We had an opportunity to meet this dynamic and brilliant poet at the reading and on several other occasions. In fact, one Sunday during his visit to New York we drove out to Scarsdale in the same car with Neruda and his wife Matilde to a luncheon that lasted well into the evening. Happily, James and Neruda felt at ease together. We met another Chilean poet, Fernando Alegría, at the luncheon. Later in the afternoon Alegría, Neruda, and James went into a quiet room and collaborated on an English translation of Neruda's "To My North American Friend." James would often recall the magical afternoon and comment that "Once I spent an entire day of my life (my life!) talking with Pablo Neruda and looking into his face."

In addition to the Neruda meeting, 1972 saw the publication of *Collected Poems*, which won the Pulitzer Prize. It is no surprise that a section of this book contains a small collection of James's translations from German and Spanish.

In 1979 James and I took an extended trip to Europe where we spent the month of June in Sirmione, the place much loved by Catullus. James couldn't have been happier. In his letters and postcards he would inform everyone where we were with this quotation by Catullus: "Paene insularum, Sirmio, insularumque ocelle" (almost an island, Sirmio, eye of islands). In a sense, after thirty-four years of working on translations, he returned to where he had begun with the Latin of Catullus.

James's life changed immensely during the fourteen years he lived in New York. He was able to recover from the stressful problems of the Minneapolis years and, thanks to AA, he stopped drinking. He became a tenured, full professor at Hunter College and continued to write three more books of poetry, his last one, *This Journey*, published posthumously. In the summers we could and often did travel to Italy and other European countries.

James never lost his love of German and Spanish poetry. Most important was the strength, determination, and courage he had gained during the many years of translation work: starting with the Latin of Catullus as a high school boy, and continuing in the Kenyon and Vienna years with German poetry and the influence in his work of contemporary poets who wrote in Spanish.

In conclusion, I'd like to quote a statement made by the poet Robert Fitzgerald, when James gave what was to be his last poetry reading at Harvard University on October 11, 1979. In his introductory remarks, Mr. Fitzgerald gave respectful praise to James, including this quote from William Carlos Williams: "James Wright is a poet in the American grain." After mentioning the titles of James's books, Mr. Fitzgerald went on to comment "Wright's translations are very fine." I believe that is high praise from a master.

In addition is one of James's last entries, written in block capitals on a yellow lined legal pad, as he could no longer speak: NERUDA FINEST SPANISH POET.

Acknowledgments

WE ARE GRATEFUL FOR the generosity of those who shared their time, materials, advice, and recollections of James Wright.

Anne Wright's gratitudes: First and foremost, I thank and acknowledge my co-authors, Saundra Maley and Jeff Katz. Saundra and I had worked happily and successfully together on *A Wild Perfection: The Selected Letters of James Wright*. When Suzanna Tamminen, director/editor-in-chief of Wesleyan University Press, suggested a book of James's translations, I agreed to do it, with Saundra as co-editor. I would work with the Spanish translations and Saundra would work with the German. In 2018, Jeffrey Katz, just retired as director of libraries at Bard College, agreed to join us. Together, their scholarship and persistent exploration of James Wright's work as a translator are what made this book possible. Our extraordinary typist, Julia Castello, deserves our special thanks.

SAUNDRA MALEY RECALLS: Some twenty years ago when I wrote the introduction for *A Wild Perfection: The Selected Letters of James Wright*, I titled it "The Great Conversation" after one of Wright's Kenyon classmates told me that Wright was at the center of the Middle Kenyon Association—the residents of a dormitory for the independent students who did not belong to a fraternity. Soon after arriving on the campus in Gambier, Ohio, on the GI Bill, Wright, older than most of his fellow students, quickly became recognized for his expansive intellect, generosity of spirit, and love of poetry. One classmate remembered that "eighty percent of what we talked about was literary. Whenever papers were to be written, and at Kenyon the discipline of writing papers was really something, especially with guys like Ransom. We were turning in a paper a week and they had to be good . . . staying up all night was routine, writing the papers and talking about the papers." These students gathered with Wright at their center in his and John Furniss's dormitory room for countless late-night discussions, carrying on their version of the Great Conversation.

I want to thank (in memory) all of the following people who helped me through interviews, letters, and telephone conversations to paint a lively picture of Wright at Kenyon: Robert Mezey, Roger Hecht, John Furniss, Nicholas Crome, Eugene Pugatch, E. L. Doctorow, Edwin Spievack, Evan Lottman, Seymour Weissman, William Goldhurst, Anthony Hecht, Albert Herzing, and Stephen Varnhagen. Herbert Lindenberger, who like Wright was on a Fulbright in Vienna in the fall of 1952, attended the same Eugene Susini seminar in which Wright discovered the poetry of Georg Trakl, and he provided firsthand knowledge of Wright's working knowledge of German and his reaction to Trakl's poetry.

Robert Bly was also helpful in describing how he and Wright approached their translations of Georg Trakl and how the translation of the German and Spanish poets affected Wright's own poetry. Merrill Leffler of Dryad Press, my teacher and mentor, gave me copies of the letters Wright had written to him as they were preparing *Moments of the Italian Summer* for publication. Merrill also sat with me on his back porch on many occasions discussing Wright's translations and poems with me. Milne Holton and Stanley Plumly were on my dissertation committee and helped me understand much of what I found in Wright's papers and in his translations, as did poet Roland Flint. Liberty Kovacs, Wright's first wife, gave me invaluable information about Wright's involvement in German translation while they were in Vienna, and his son Franz Wright, born during that Fulbright year and a poet himself (and a translator of Rilke), exchanged letters with me when I wrote him about his work with his father when they published Hesse's *Selected Poems*. And finally, thanks to Jeffrey Katz, without whose "secret labor" this two-legged work would not have seen completion. His devotion to Wright's poetry, as well as his deep understanding and articulation of Wright's creative process, pulled this book into a balanced whole.

As always, none of this would have been possible without the support and encouragement of Anne Wright.

JEFF KATZ'S GRATITUDES: I thank my wife Mary for her unfailing support, expertise and careful attention to every detail of text and image, and for her willingness to "begin again" with every false start and draft. For their enthusiastic support and for perceptive readings of earlier drafts of the manuscript, I thank Jeff Schwartz, Pam Neides, Emily Katz, and Lawrence Kramer. I would also like to acknowledge my debt to William H. Roberson, whose indispensable *James Wright: An Annotated Bibliography* guided us through much of the publication history of Wright's translations.

WE ARE ALL ESPECIALLY INDEBTED to the scores of library staff who inventoried, organized, and described James Wright's original papers at Chalmers Library Special Collections and Archives at Kenyon College. We wish particularly to thank Librarian Allan Bosch and Thomas Boardman Greenslade, archivist, and their staffs, who welcomed and guided us in our research. Great thanks also to the cheerful and indispensable staff of the Upper Midwest Literary Archives (UMLA) at Elmer L. Andersen Library, University of Minnesota, the current home of the Wright Papers, and in particular to Pearl McClintock, collections associate, and to Erin McBrien, interim UMLA curator, for her crucial work on securing many of the images that form the book's core. We are also grateful to Ruth and Mary Bly for permission to quote from Robert Bly's letters and from collaborative translations.

Many thanks, too, to Suzanna Tamminen, editor-in-chief of Wesleyan University Press, for her enthusiastic support of the project, and to our editorial team, Jim Schley and Ally Findley, for handling the manuscript with great skill and sensitivity at every step along the way.

Introduction: James Wright and the Sound of the Human Voice

JEFFREY KATZ

> I haven't included all the translations I've made because translations have meant so much to me and to so many other poets that the intrusion of so much secret labor would be an indiscretion.
>
> Excerpt of a draft entitled "To the Reader"[1]

WHEN JAMES WRIGHT LET HIMSELF down into the deep shaft of a poem by Rainer Maria Rilke or César Vallejo for weeks at a time, he was right where he wanted to be. He hardly ate or slept. It was essential to him that he was not simply reading the poems in the original language, but translating them.

So Much Secret Labor describes Wright's long engagement with translation. It does so not by taking up, again, the vexed question of what makes a good literary translation, but rather by providing a rich context of materials from various sources to answer the more pertinent question: Why was translating poems so important to Wright's life and his practice? What treasure did he find there?

Together Anne Wright and Saundra Maley present a scrupulous and affectionate reading of James Wright's life and work that shows him in the midst of the translations he insisted were as redemptive in his life as they were crucial to his poetics.

The poet gives us some idea early on of the ways translation work was so important to him in several unpublished letters from the late 1950s: "I can't afford to buy the complete works of Jiménez and yet I need them so terribly, the way a man needs water . . ."[2] About Vallejo he writes: ". . . I owe him so much, because he reminded me that perhaps I too might somehow vindicate myself, not only as an artist but even as a man."[3] Again about Jiménez he writes: ". . . the poet I am translating is so great, so huge, so humane and original! I feel as if great doors were opening in me all the time."[4] Attached to a translation of Lorca's poem "Malagueña" in a letter from 1959 is an urgent description of a key element of Wright's developing aesthetic, his project, his ethic: "Oh, if only I could learn it. They have dropped all the rhetoric and gone straight to the truth of the soul itself and insisted that the heart is true, that we have no right to reason it away, and they can drop the rhetoric (which I have so often used as a mere defense against experience) because they are not afraid."[5] He needed these voices; he needed their fearlessness; he needed the edge they put on his own language.

Wright worked continuously on translations beginning with high school translations of Catullus in Martins Ferry, Ohio, until shortly before his death in New York City in 1980. At Kenyon College (1948–1951) he discovered German poets—Rilke, Heinrich Heine, Hermann Hesse, Friedrich Hölderlin, and Theodor Storm, among many others. His papers at the University of Minnesota contain hundreds of draft translations from the German during this period. In fact, in the summer after his first year at Kenyon he created a collection of his poems, *Folio for Summer, 1949*, giving a central place to a group of fourteen translations he called *Imitations and Adaptations from the German*. In 1958 Wright began working with Robert Bly on the translations that would introduce poets such as Georg Trakl, Pablo Neruda, Vallejo, and Juan Ramón Jiménez to his contemporaries and to the American poetry reading public of the 1960s and 1970s. But his serious engagement with the German poets had begun ten years before. In chapter 2, "A Solitary Apprenticeship: The German Poets," Saundra Maley provides the detailed background for this critical but largely unknown early period of his German apprenticeship.

"If you try to translate [the poems]," he told Bruce Hendrickson in an interview in *New Orleans Review*, "you are forced to find some equivalents in your own language, not only equivalents in language itself but equivalents of imagination."[6] This notion of "finding equivalents of imagination" is the key principle animating *So Much Secret Labor.* James Wright was not a linguist; he was a seeker. He was seeking an imagination equal to the effort to "enter and to recognize one's very self," as he writes of Trakl's poetry.[7] The only worthy goal of the human effort of poetry, he writes in "Meditations on René Char," "is the search for reality, the desire to embrace it without taking it prisoner."[8] In the best of his poems, one feels that everything is at stake, that every effort strains to "enter and recognize one's very self." It was the same with the translations. He wanted something from them, but not the perfect English version of a German poem. He didn't want to own the German or Spanish poems on which he worked so diligently. He wanted to live in the hope these poets gave him, in their example, of the discipline required not to demonstrate reality, but to embrace it fearlessly.

Wright published translations throughout his career, including an early contribution of translations of Char, in *Hypnos Waking: Poetry and Prose of René Char* (Random House, 1956), and four individual volumes of German translations: *Twenty Poems of Georg Trakl* (with Robert Bly, Sixties Press, 1961), *The Rider on the White Horse* by Theodor Storm (New American Library, 1964), *Poems* by Hermann Hesse (Farrar, Straus and Giroux, 1970), and *Wanderings: Notes and Sketches* by Hermann Hesse (with his teenage son Franz Wright, Noonday Press, 1972). He also contributed Spanish translations to individual volumes produced with Robert Bly, for instance *Twenty Poems of Pablo Neruda* (Sixties Press, 1962) and *Twenty Poems of César Vallejo* (with Bly and John Knoepfle, Sixties Press, 1962). He published five brief but important critical essays introducing his translations of René Char (1956), Georg Trakl (1963), César Vallejo (1963), Theodor Storm (1964), and Hermann Hesse (1970). These are gathered in *Collected Prose*, edited by Anne Wright (University of Michigan Press, 1983). *So Much Secret Labor* includes a selected bibliography of Wright's published translations in individual volumes, his critical writing related to translation, and important secondary sources, for instance interviews and letters in which translation figures prominently.

The evidence that Anne Wright and Saundra Maley provide in

their detailed history shows that Wright's translation work was a major force, early and late, in shaping his own poems. Recognition of the importance of translation to the development of Wright's work has largely rested on the crucial Spanish-language poets and a single Austrian poet, Georg Trakl. In chapter 2, Saundra Maley completes, for the first time, the picture of Wright's early and intense engagement with German poetry, particularly Rilke and Heine. She traces the ways tone, cadence, and imagery begin migrating from the translations into the poems he was writing in the 1950s that became *The Green Wall* and *Saint Judas*, an influence that would continue through his final volumes, *To a Blossoming Pear Tree* and *This Journey*.

Chapter 3, "A Fine Weave of Voices: Whitman, Translation, and James Wright's New Style," describes the crucial years 1958–1961 that bring the voices of Whitman, Trakl, and Vallejo together with Wright's intense examination alongside Robert Bly of the situation of American postwar poetry. At the same time Wright was making dozens of translations, he was also making dozens of drafts of the poems that would make up *The Branch Will Not Break* (1963). Under a kind of tidal influence provided by the translations—both deep and delightful—*The Branch* and his next book *Shall We Gather at the River* (1968) became the new north around which his own work revolved— more open, more urgent, and more restless.

So Much Secret Labor makes extensive use of memoir, archival research, interviews, letters, and previously unpublished journal excerpts, putting in context the critical significance of translation work in James Wright's poetry, his life, and the life of American poetry in the 1960s and 1970s.

At this book's center is a selection of Wright's translations from both German and Spanish, representing work published in edited volumes and journals from the 1950s, 1960s, and 1970s, as well as draft versions discovered among his collected papers that have never been published. In all, seventy-two translations are included, representing sixteen poets. Particularly interesting is a significant section of German translations of Rilke, Heine, and Storm—all early translations and what Wright called adaptations or imitations, most of which have never been published. Chapter 5, "Here is Nourishment," contains several of Wright's earliest drafts of translations of the Peruvian poet César Vallejo found in unpublished letters and journals. The final versions of these poems are included in the "Selected Spanish Translations" section, along with other Vallejo poems and a selection of long out-of-print, uncollected, and unpublished translations of Federico García Lorca, Neruda, Miguel Hernández, Jorge Guillén, and Juan Ramón Jiménez.

Chapter 7, "Georg Trakl's 'Grodek' Translated by James Wright and Robert Bly: A Portfolio," looks over the shoulders of Wright and Bly as they work at the translation of Trakl's seventeen-line war poem "Grodek." It presents the work as the exchange of a series of heavily annotated handwritten drafts, letters, and journal entries.

Whether James Wright was listening to a ravishing line of Rilke, a favorite country song like Roy Acuff's "Great Speckled Bird," or a scratchy LP of Heine's *lieder*, he says with Whitman: "I hear the sound I love, the sound of the human voice."

Wright's devotion to translation, working from the inside of other poetic voices, gave him access to the new kind of poetry which he was ardently seeking. These poets opened a door to a poetry of emotional urgency and transparency that he felt stripped away mere elegance and discursiveness. These poems shine like a bright path through the entire body of his work.

So Much Secret Labor completes the work Anne Wright began with the publication of *Above the River: The Complete Poems of James Wright* (1990). With the advice of friends, colleagues, and editors, the project has moved through nearly thirty years of gathering James Wright's brave and brilliant work as poet, translator, teacher, and critic for a new generation of readers.

James Wright Among Other Voices: A Chronology

JEFFREY KATZ

1927   James Arlington Wright is born on December 13 in Martins Ferry, Ohio: "I had lived in all the neighborhoods except the wealthy ones," he writes in "Childhood Sketch,"[1] ". . . and I knew most of the languages [Greek, Polish, Hungarian, Welsh], and carry with me today the affections of those words."

1942–1945   Attends Shreve High School, Martins Ferry, Ohio, where he studies both Latin and Spanish in his junior and senior year; first translates Horace and Catullus.

1946   Joins the US Army and is stationed in Japan. Writes to Elizabeth Willerton, his high school English teacher: "My longing for Latin is deeper than ever now, since I have assembled a vocabulary large enough to read the beautiful volume of Catullus not only with pleasure, but with a great deal of fire."

1948–1952   Attends Kenyon College where he studies German with Frederic Eberle and Andre Hanfman and poetic analysis with John Crowe Ransom; immerses himself in Rilke, Heine, Mörike, Goethe, and Hesse, among others.

1949   Produces *Folio for Summer, 1949*, a collection of his first poems, giving a central place to a group of fourteen translations he called *Imitations and Adaptations from the German*, including first versions of one of the Rilke poems most important to a recurrent theme in his own work: "Orpheus. Eurydike. Hermes."

1950   A notebook entry shows a translation of the funeral passage in *Beowulf* along with a version of Rilke's "A Picture of My Father in His Youth," and an important early poem of his own "Father," published by Ransom in *The Kenyon Review* (1951).

1952   Receives Fulbright Scholarship to travel to Vienna, Austria; wanders into the classroom of Professor Eugene Susini and stays for his series of lectures on Georg Trakl.

1954   Attends the University of Washington to study with Theodore Roethke; produces a student portfolio which includes a substantial selection of Trakl translations and notes on metrics.

1955   Joins faculty at the University of Minnesota; works with a colleague there, poet Sarah Youngblood, on a small collection, never published, of Rilke translations that includes the pivotal late Rilke poem, "Christi Höllenfahrt."

1956   Wins the Yale Younger Poets Prize for *The Green Wall*; contributes three translations to a new version of René Char's *Hypnos Waking*, which also featured translations by Jackson Matthews, William Carlos Williams, and Richard Wilbur.

1958   Begins correspondence and vital friendship with Robert Bly, who has said, "I think that I brought Neruda to Jim, and he brought a lot of Rilke and new Trakl to me."

1959   *Saint Judas* is published by Wesleyan University Press. Undertakes deep and sustained work on translation: Trakl, Vallejo, Jiménez, Neruda, and Guillén.

1961   Bly's Sixties Press publishes *Twenty Poems of Georg Trakl*, with translations by Bly and Wright.

1961   English Institute presentation of "The Delicacy of Walt Whitman," Columbia University.

1962   Sixties Press publishes *Twenty Poems of César Vallejo*, with translations by Wright, Bly, and John Knoepfle.

1963	*The Branch Will Not Break* is published by Wesleyan University Press; translation of Theodor Storm's *The Rider on the White Horse* is published by New American Library (E. L. Doctorow, editor).
1968	*Shall We Gather at the River* is published by Wesleyan University Press; Sixties Press publishes *Twenty Poems of Pablo Neruda*, with translations by Bly and Wright.
1970	Translation of *Poems* by Hermann Hesse is published by Farrar, Straus and Giroux.
1971	*Collected Poems* is published by Wesleyan University Press and wins the Pulitzer Prize for Poetry; the volume includes twenty-nine translations from German and Spanish. Also translates, with son Franz, *Wandering* by Hermann Hesse.
1972	Travels by car with Anne, Pablo Neruda, and Neruda's wife Matilde to a lunch in Scarsdale, New York, with Chilean poet Fernando Alegría. Later, Wright recalled: "And once I spent an entire day of my life (my life!) talking with Pablo Neruda and looking into his face."
1979	With Annie visits Sirmione, Italy, the long green peninsula that stretches into Lake Garda, and in a letter recalls "a little poem [by Catullus] printed toward the back of Miss Sheriff's old beginner's text in Latin. It begins 'Paene insularum, Sirmio, insularumque ocelle . . .'"
1980	James Wright dies at Calvary Hospital, The Bronx, New York.
1983	The James Wright papers arrive at the Olin-Chalmers Library at Kenyon College. In 1992 they are acquired by the Elmer L. Andersen Library at the University of Minnesota, Minneapolis. The papers include correspondence from more than a hundred different correspondents, carbons he kept of those letters, his personal journals and notebooks, loose drafts of published and unpublished poems and manuscripts, and many, many drafts of individual poems and translations.

1983	*Collected Prose*, edited by Anne Wright, is published by the University of Michigan Press, containing five important essays on the work of René Char, Theodor Storm, Georg Trakl, César Vallejo, and Hermann Hesse, as well as *Some Notes on Chinese Poetry*.
1990	*Above the River: The Complete Poems of James Wright* expands the selection of translations by thirteen, including addition of poems by Hermann Hesse and Miguel Hernández, and from the Yiddish of Aleph Katz.
2005	*A Wild Perfection: The Selected Letters of James Wright*, edited by Anne Wright and Saundra Rose Maley, is published by Farrar, Straus and Giroux, containing many letters about Catullus, Char, Rilke, Trakl, Vallejo, and Neruda, among others.

Note: The sources for many of these dates and descriptions are Saundra Rose Maley's *Solitary Apprenticeship: James Wright and German Poetry* and Jonathan Blunk's *James Wright: A Life in Poetry*.

So Much Secret Labor

1. First Translations

ANNE WRIGHT

JAMES WRIGHT'S INTEREST in the poetry of Catullus was stimulated by Helen McNeely Sheriff, his Latin teacher at the Martins Ferry High School when, at the age of seventeen or eighteen, he began to translate the work of Catullus. James's devotion to that poet, along with what he chose to translate from the work of Catullus, occupied him for many years.

The first letter in *A Wild Perfection*, dated 1946, is to Professor James L. McCreight, who had been introduced to him by Elizabeth Willerton, his high school English teacher. James thanked him for his gift of a volume of poems by Catullus and went on to comment that when he discovered Catullus, "the white gush of nobility in his lines ate at me considerably. Perhaps his ability to create poetic images could not approach that of Virgil, or even that of the more sensible Horace, but his cries—

nam tui Catulli
Plenus sacculus est aranearum.

—charged me with such a weird hunger, such as that created by Chopin or Poe."[1]

I found his flowery prose was unusual for a young man of eighteen, but then how many eighteen-year-olds are involved in poetry, let alone the art of translation, especially from the Latin?

IN JANUARY OF 1947 James sent a letter from Zama, Japan, to Elizabeth Willerton, his former English teacher and mentor. The message was completely about the translation.

Dear Elizabeth,

Tonight I felt lousy therefore I turned to Catullus for a sea in which to drown. This lyric (other side), an ode by a very sensitive and young poet to Lesbia's pet sparrow, is the first paraphrase I have attempted in weeks. I tell you, Catullus is as dear to me as sleep and music.

Please look for neither ecstasy nor a moral in my paraphrase. It is only a softly mournful remark, and the Latin is unspeakably gorgeous. Catullus therein created a line which sings thus:

Et solaciolum sui doloris.

Elizabeth, read this line aloud. The relationship between the "i's" and the "o's" is a miracle of liquid floating ecstasy.

Forgive me. I told you my mood was crazy again.

The lights are going out.

I shall not sleep well. Catullus and I are pacing the floor.

Love,
Jim[2]

On the other side of the letter was this lyric.

ODE TO LESBIA'S PET SPARROW

Sparrow of my love's delight,
    Feathered soul of airiest flight
Whom she has blest against her breast
    In warmth, she felt her fingers prest
Surely upon your soft light wing—:

When she will listen as I sing
    The barbed pain of my desire,
And laugh, as though love's aching fire

Could never touch her, make her wear
Gem-like one single feminine tear

Then she will jest as easily
With you, as in my torment, I
Attempt to salve in sleep the smart
Of bruised longing in my heart.

When he was in the army, he continued his work with transla-
tions. In addition to correspondence with Elizabeth Willerton, he
also wrote to Susan Lamb, a classmate from Martins Ferry. In a letter
dated September 3, 1946, he mentioned his devotion to that work.

> Just before I came in the army, I wrestled with many translations
> which I had already completed, and with a few that I somehow
> had missed, endeavoring to retain in English a larger share of
> Catullus's spirit by utilizing his own favorite metre.[3]

The journey from a working-class town in Martins Ferry, Ohio to a
lakeside town in Sirmione, Italy was long and complicated. But, when
he was an older man, he and I made three trips there and, in 1979,
stayed for a month. That long visit was a delight for both of us. I was
happy to join James as we explored the peninsula and swam below
the cliff where the alleged villa of Catullus lay in romantic ruin. He
worked so well in such a peaceful and beautiful setting.
During that last visit he wrote to Tom Hodge, an old school friend
from Martins Ferry:

> I wonder if you remember a little poem printed toward the back
> of Miss Sheriff's old beginner's text in Latin. It begins "Paene
> insularum, Sirmio, insularumque ocelle . . ." (almost an island,
> Sirmio, eye of islands). The lines are by the ancient Roman
> Catullus. He used to come to this place in the summer, to visit
> friends at a villa whose ruins lie in an olive grove on a cliff way
> up at the tip of the peninsula, to rest there, no doubt (if his other
> poems are to be believed) from a strenuous life in Rome.[4]

I feel the particular stimulation and recognition given to James by his two high school teachers, Elizabeth Willerton Esterly and Helen McNeely Sheriff, helped lead to his intense early work of translation. He never lost touch with these early mentors. He visited Elizabeth and her husband Henry Esterly in California and continued to correspond with them. In the late 1970s, during a visit to Ted and Helen Wright in Zanesville, Ohio, we were invited to dinner at Miss Sheriff's family home in Cadiz. She not only remembered the exact place where James had sat in her classroom over twenty years ago, but both former teacher and student talked together as if it had been yesterday.

To A Blossoming Pear Tree (1977) is dedicated to Miss Sheriff. In the poem "Piccolini," from that book, he writes of Catullus:

> Catullus, grieving over his Lesbia's sparrow, turned
> *misere* from harsh wretched in *miselle*, poor
> and little lovely and gone, all in one word.

And in *This Journey*, published posthumously in 1982, he writes once more of Sirmione in "At the End of Sirmione":

> And Sirmione, here, the lizard of cisterns, turning
> Silver as olive in the underside of rain
> That leaves me alone in the cliff's grotto, anything
> But cold.

As a young man, James Wright made his declaration about the poetry of Catullus and the poet himself: "His songs are pure gold, and he will live forever."[5] I believe the songs and spirit of Catullus did continue to live in James Wright's heart then and during the rest of his life.

2. A Solitary Apprenticeship:
The German Poets

SAUNDRA ROSE MALEY

> And I love to read a James Wright poem.
> He is our best singer.
>
> —Steve Orlen, in *Ironwood* (1977)[1]

I was introduced to James Wright's poetry in the late 1960s in a course on poetics at the University of Maryland. I still have the dittoed sheet Rod Jellema handed out to the class, and, although the strangely medicinal aroma has faded from the paper, my memory of how Wright's poems jumped off that page has not—I was drawn to those poems by what felt like a magnetic force. Years later, when I chose Wright as the subject of my dissertation, shortly after his death, I was to discover the extent of the energy behind that force.

When I first started my exploration of Wright and translation, I had intended to focus on his Spanish translations, but early on, Merrill Leffler, editor of Dryad Press (and publisher of Wright's *Moments of the Italian Summer*), gave me a copy of the journal *Ironwood*, a special issue devoted to Wright. In that tribute, the late poet and scholar Steve Orlen wrote an essay on Wright's first book of poetry, *The Green Wall*, in which he made an astute and surprising observation about a kinship he saw between Wright and the German poet, Rilke:

Given the irrepressibility of his later work, how odd it is to see this young poet walking in Frost's shoes, in Frost's meters. I also see, walking beside, the almost too exquisite vulnerability of Rainer Maria Rilke.[2]

Orlen's comment immediately made me curious about Wright's possible interest in Rilke, a German-language poet. I went back and searched through Wright's published works and found no sign of Rilke, but I did begin to find a number of German footprints and I decided to follow their path. Orlen was right.

So, the journey began.

JAMES WRIGHT'S EARLY CAREER displays one of the most rigorous apprenticeships of any American poet since World War II. He, indeed, apprenticed himself not only to British and American poetry, but to a body of German literature in the years before his better-known encounters with Spanish literature. For the most part, Wright's early German translations were not for publication, they were openings that led him to the creation of his own poems—apprenticeship by translation. For years Wright's debt to Spanish-language poets of the twentieth century has been acknowledged, and linked to Wright's association with Robert Bly. The influence of Georg Trakl also has been recognized, but never with the understanding of the early and extensive knowledge and translation of German poetry that he brought to his initial encounter with Trakl's poetry in Vienna and later to his friendship with Robert Bly.

Given the large number of German translations among Wright's papers, we must reconsider our understanding of his poetry, his approach to translation, and its dramatic effect on his own poems. Wright found in these foreign models the kind of poetry he wanted to write, and that was everything to him. When he decided, as an undergraduate, to translate German poetry at a time when Germany was internationally unpopular, he revealed his sense of poetic integrity. Despite the opprobrium in which Germany was held following World War II, the music of German poetry drew him to it, and he followed. His brooding personality made him especially receptive to the often dark poems of the Germans, whose themes of alienation, solitude, and death were subjects he was exploring in his earliest poems. "Einsamkeit" (solitude or loneliness), the wandering and seeking of German poets, their intense emotionalism and mystical approach to nature, all serve to characterize Wright's own poetic sensibility. In the German and Spanish poems, Wright found what he was looking for—words and images that would "lash his eyes open."

He published German translations throughout his career alongside his own work. He placed eight untranslated lines from Heine as an epigraph for *The Branch Will Not Break* (1963), and another from Theodor Storm introduces the breakthrough ars poetica of the volume, "Goodbye to the Poetry of Calcium." A translation of three stanzas from Goethe's "Harzreise im Winter" is also in that important book. His *Collected Poems* (1971) includes five poems of Trakl's, and Goethe's "Anacreon's Grave." He published many translations in magazines from his undergraduate days throughout the seventies, and included others in manuscripts of proposed volumes.

In fact, the James Wright Papers, now permanently housed at the University of Minnesota (https://archives.lib.umn.edu/repositories/16 /resources/577), contain hundreds of drafts of translations from nearly one hundred works, including poems by: Rainer Maria Rilke (1875– 1926), Heinrich Heine (1797–1856), Theodor Storm (1817–1888), Walther von der Vogelweide (ca. 1170–1230), Johann Wolfgang von Goethe (1749–1832), Johann Christian Friedrich Hölderlin (1770–1843), Friedrich von Hardenberg [Novalis] (1772–1801), Joseph von Eichendorff, August (1788–1857), Graf von Platen-Hallermünde (1796–1835), Nikolaus Lenau (1802–1850), Eduard Mörike (1804–1875), Friedrich Wilhelm Nietzsche (1844–1900), Richard Dehmel (1863–1920), Hugo von Hofmannsthal (1874–1929), Hans Carossa (1878–1956), and Hermann Hesse (1877–1962). He would discover Georg Trakl (1887–1914) on a Fulbright scholarship in Vienna in 1952.

Wright's close study and translation of these poets began when he was an undergraduate at Kenyon College on the GI Bill, and they had a considerable technical and thematic influence on his work throughout his career. This can be seen in his agile associative imagery, his directness and humor—on his very sense of the ways a poem could work. Themes that have come to be associated with Wright's work—the presence of the working poor, loneliness, homesickness, a deep relationship to nature, childhood, the Orphic voice, the Eurydice figure, and sudden illumination—often have antecedents in the German poems with which he spent so much time.

The notebooks Wright kept his whole life, especially those of his early years, clearly show drafts of many translations moving right off the page from rough versions into his own poems. One instance of his movement from Rilke translation work into the beginnings of an important original poem can be found among his undergraduate papers. Wright may have had the poems of Rilke's *Book of Poverty and Death* (Book III of *Das Stundenbuch*) about the hidden lives of the urban poor in which "Cities turn their forces full on their own" in mind as he worked on his own rich, raw Ohio poems:

> George Doty killed a girl one night because
> She would not lay for him inside his car.
> My friend Daub Meyer took a wife in June,
> And died last month before he had a son.
> I had another friend who liked to sleep
> With little boys, and so he killed himself.
> The birds directly die, the leaves are dead.
> God, on the other hand, is still alive.

He jotted down these early lines of a poem about George Doty, the Ohio Valley rapist and murderer, executed in 1951, who figures in two of his best-known and most controversial poems: "A Poem about George Doty in the Death House," first published in 1955 in the *Paris Review*[3] and then in *The Green Wall* (1957), and "At the Executed Murderer's Grave, published in *Saint Judas* (1959).

Wright was a serious student of German language and literature at Kenyon College. Books in the library collection there still have his signature on check-out cards for early Rilke volumes, *Frühen Gedichte* (*Early Poems*) and *Erste Gedichte* (*First Poems*). He took every German

2.1 An early draft of "A Poem about George Doty in the Death House," first published in 1955 in the *Paris Review* as "A Complaint for George Doty in the Death House," then in Wright's first book, *The Green Wall*.

course the college had to offer, simultaneously studying the language and the poetry. His study of the German language began under the direction of Frederic "Cap" Eberle, a teacher described by one of Wright's classmates as "a blustering Baron von Munchhausen" who drilled his students mercilessly in the mechanics of grammar. When he enrolled in Intermediate German, Wright met the teacher who had the greatest influence on him in regard to German, Andre Hanf-man, professor of modern languages. E. L. Doctorow, another Kenyon classmate of Wright's, described Hanfman as a "multi-lingual Russian émigré who must have been astounded by the farm boy/poet, so serious and so gifted, and built like a nose tackle."[4] Years after leaving Kenyon, Wright recalled in a letter how Hanfman had brought German to life for him:

> His brilliance as a teacher was hair-raising . . . As long as I live
> I will never forget how, a good three weeks after Dr. Hanfman
> had begun his course in Goethe, I found myself walking across
> the campus and being delighted in German.[5]

Wright's first sustained efforts at translation were the untranslated *Frühen Gedichte* (*Early Poems*) and *Erste Gedichte* (*First Poems*) of Rilke. Wright dove into the originals and devoted many hours to reworking and revising his translations. Kenyon classmates and fellow poets Robert Mezey and Nicholas Crome enthusiastically remarked on Wright's love of the sound of German poetry. Eugene Pugatch, a fellow Kenyonite and lifelong friend, remembers first meeting Wright in the Peirce Hall Music Room, Wright listening to a rendition of Goethe's "Erlkönig," following along with the lyrics in *The Oxford Book of German Verse*. Classmates Seymour Weissman and Ed Spievack recalled how Wright would recite long German passages from memory. Spievack vividly remembered Wright bursting into a room, booming "Listen to this Rilke, listen to the sound of it."[6]

During his second summer vacation from Kenyon, after the day's work of helping out on his parents' Warnock farm, Wright worked feverishly on a 193-page manuscript of poetry he called the "Folio for Summer, 1949." At the center of that collection is a section of fourteen of his earliest German translations, which he called "Imitations and Adaptations." Even at this early stage in his writing life, Wright signaled his attitude about translation. Twenty years later he would prepare a similar central collection of twenty-nine translations for his *Collected Poems*. His very earliest writing puts German translations right next to his own poems. In fact, his practice in this period was more like bringing Rilke's lines into his own, as if to write through them, almost as a young musician might work through the night perfecting cover versions of the songs of her heroes.

What the young poet ended up doing was creating a scene of initiation, of instruction, of the commissioning of his poetic vocation by Rilke. Together, his adaptations of Rilke's "Ich war ein Kind und träumte viel" ("I was a child and dreamed a lot"), which he called "Ghost with a Silver Lyre," and the dark, longer poem he ultimately called "Vision and Elegy" narrate the founding story of Wright's poetry.

"Ich war ein Kind" tells the story (or the dream) of a child whose imagination is captivated by a strange man with a lyre passing by. "At the first sound of his lyre," the speaker says, "something broke in two for me." Wright's translation of the poem emphasizes the strangeness of the music, both the allure and the threat, and the intimation of a kind of sacrifice to come.

> I knew even before his song began:
> that it would be my life.
> Sing not, sing not, you strange man:
> It will be my life.
>
> *translation by Saundra Rose Maley*

In fact, Wright's marginalia, in what is probably the first handwritten literal version of this imitation, indicates his thoughts on the implications of the important line, "Es wird mein Leben sein":

> It will be my life: (it will mean my life? both life and death in a phrase) [Wright's underline]. That is, poetry will become what I live for AND it will require my life. The deeply ambivalent speaker of the poem is under the threat of his own disappearance (as a social person), and yet the remembered lyre: ". . . throbbed and throbbed through my imaginings, / And lit the core of my own ghost with fire."[7]

In the end, the stranger and his strange song travel on, but the song is now become part of the boy:

> He sang. And then his step died away—
> he had to travel on
> and sang my song that I would never suffer,
> and sang my happiness that escaped me,
> and took me along, and took me along—
> and no one knows where to . . .
>
> *translation by Saundra Rose Maley*

In a letter that summer, Wright tells his Kenyon roommate Jack Furniss about his "new folio of verses," and adds that he was "having a fine time, trying to read the Grimm's fairy tales in German."[8] Warnock became the setting for his continuing study of German and the writing of his own poems. In another letter to Furniss, he complained:

> Every evening at eleven or so I further work on my new folio of verses . . . all I do at night now is sit and worry over a long elegiac thing which won't clear itself up. It is hideously difficult to apply a critical technique to this raw, rich Ohioan material.[9]

The "long elegiac thing" to which Wright refers in this letter is a strange, ambitious 162-line poem he worked at through many drafts and eventually published in *Hika*, the Kenyon College literary journal, as "Vision and Elegy" in 1950. Although previous versions of the poem had included many lines from Rilke, often in German, the final version eliminates these German lines in favor of references to Rilke's poems by way of establishing him as the tutelary spirit of the poet's voice.

"Vision and Elegy" continues the story of Wright's "self-fashioning" as a poet, which he began in his "Ghost with the Silver Lyre." The world of "Vision and Elegy" is a dark, insubstantial world of remnants, ghosts, mists, and shadows. It is an autumnal world but just on the hard edge of winter, of dark, wind-clawed trees, barrenness, rotten apples, sore wounds, vacuous and imaginary light. In short, the "world of sad repair" of the poem's epigraph from Lenau, a world with neither a consoling past nor a promising future. The poem's dark landscape may in fact owe more to Germans other than Rilke, more to Lenau and Novalis whom he also translated, or the Grimm brothers, whom he was reading at the time; more to melancholia, or even torment, than to the deep yearning of Rilke's monk.

But Rilke is the poet here who authorizes the speaker to begin speaking:

> I touched the pages and began again
> To chant the quiet music of the gods
> In German, something about a little death . . .
>
> How he was only the bearer of a word
> I knew once as a child, but had forgotten . . .

A few lines later Wright includes lines from Rilke's *Das Stundenbuch*, which he had been translating: "Mein Leben ist nicht diese steile Stunde"—"My life is not this steep hour," a beautiful image in which he imagines the relationship of death to the ongoing song:

> As though to die were nothing but the last
> Breath one may take, or else the final note
> Of a string work one builds upon the past . . .

Although Wright did not complete his translation of "Mein Leben ist nicht," the final lines of this important short poem are clearly the source. His translation of the poem, which he called "Out of Rilke," ends like this:

> I am the rest between two tones:
> Together they would shatter out of key,
> Because the sound of death would raise up one.
> But in the darkened interval of me

They meet.
    And so the lovely song goes on.

In his imagination the poet builds a place—an altar, perhaps a memorial—for Rilke in his imagination from sea and wind:

> The wind wiped long loose fringes of foam away
> From the shore's edge below, and set a gray
> Disturbance shocking along wires of cloud,
> That knit the sky together like a shroud.
> This was the place for Rilke.

Rilke's ghost appears throughout the remainder of the poem and quotes another line from the lovely "Mein Leben is nicht . . ." as a final lesson to the speaker: "I am a tree before my own background," that is, against what has come before and what will vanish, I am deeply rooted, sustained by song. As Rilke's ghost disappears,

> The wind drew back his ghost into the sea.
> The wind drew back my ghost into the lake.
> The morning twilight faded off my lake;
> And voices at its edges were awake,
> To lead me home by sound.[10]

Yet, what characterizes the speaker of "Vision and Elegy"? Anxiety, threat, vigilance, suffering. While the Rilke poems in Book One of *The Book of Hours* are vividly aspirational, "Vision and Elegy" is not. It takes autumn as its season, though not the ripening or readiness characteristic of early autumn, but the darkening and hardening of approaching winter. Time in this world is a kind of dream-time, not a longed-for past or a promising future, but a fragmented, ghostly present of receding, withdrawing, dying voices—a chaotic landscape.

Ultimately, the voices joining Rilke's in the poem's final thirty lines lead the speaker home, but the achievement seems incomplete, the closing of the poem vague and unsatisfying. It's almost as if "Vision and Elegy" were the first of two movements. The first (the one we have) is the experience of a Holy Fire, but the second movement, the courage and faith to live day by day, was waiting to be written.

Wright made dozens of translations of Rilke's early poems, but he also knew the poet's more mature works, especially the two volumes of *Neue Gedichte* (*New Poems*, 1907 and 1908). Among these, perhaps "Orpheus. Eurydike. Hermes." can be said to be the most important to him, because the poem explores two subjects that become most vital to his work in the years to come: the unreachable beloved and the limits of poetic knowledge. (See "Selected German Translations.")

Wright's translation of "Orpheus. Eurydike. Hermes" was the result of many drafts at the time he was putting together his summer portfolio in 1949, although it never appeared in that manuscript. In Rilke's Orpheus, Wright found a singer of great power and even greater sadness. He hears a founding story of poetic knowledge that emphasizes its insufficiency to effect its greatest desire—the rescue of the beloved. His song to her recreates heaven and earth in the image of his sorrow, here in his own translation:

> And a whole world came out of its long wailing,
> In which all things existed: valley and forest,
> Village and path, field and river and beast;
> And she was for that wailing world entirely
> As for the other earth a sun may be,
> Along with which a starry heaven goes,
> A mournful heaven with disfigured stars—:
> She who was so beloved.[11]

Yet Orpheus, who can sing a world of which Eurydice is the center, cannot bring her home with him. One of the many questions of this heartbreaking poem is about the limits of poetic knowledge or the redemptive power of art. It is a question that Rilke and Wright return to again and again. Wright worked on many poems in his undergraduate years on the theme of the singer's power and ambition, including two translations of Rilke's *Sonnets to Orpheus* II and III from Book One. Both poems deal with the question of what a poem can do, what a poem can make happen.

> A god is lucky enough. But tell me, how
> Should a man follow him through the slender lyre?
> . . .
> Song is not craving, as you teach it me,
> Not wooing what is found upon the road.
> Song is being. Easy for the god.
> But when can *we* exist?[12]
>
> *Wright's translation, from* Sonnets to Orpheus *II and III*

But what can a poem make *happen* is exactly the wrong question, Rilke seems to say: "Your desire for transcendence, for ecstasy, for salvation—all that passionate music—gets in the way of true singing. It will all vanish. The song of your youth is one kind of thing, an instrument, an achievement, but true singing comes from listening." Throughout his life, Wright was both devoted to poetry and attentive to its limits, mindful of its constant swerving.

The speaker asks about the Eurydice figure: Where is her death? She has achieved something in her death that is outside the song, the song that will consume itself. It cannot stop her from vanishing. She is "Ein Mädchen fast," a girl almost, but something entirely new. She is as the earlier Orpheus poem suggests now "deep within herself," and in her death "filled beyond fulfillment." Wright would deal many times in his poetry over the years with a vanishing, unrecoverable beloved and with the limits of poetry. It's all we have, he seems to say, but it's never enough.

This is the moment Wright turns his attention through Orpheus and toward the Eurydice figure, a sustaining energy, the highest hypothesis of desire. In a poem called "The Quest," written a few years after these Rilke translations and published in the *New Yorker* (October 30, 1954), Wright brings together the various strains of Rilke and his own struggle with "Vision and Elegy" into a work more fluid, more open, and more subtle. Although it was not included in *The Green Wall* (1957), it was one of two poems placed at the head of his

Collected Poems (1971) and provides a critical transit between the earlier poems, adaptations, and translations, and the fine new poems he began writing and publishing in the early 1950s such as "Eleutheria," "Father," "Elegy in a Firelit Room," and "The Horse."

In "The Quest," Wright revisits the fragmented, attenuated world of "Vision and Elegy." The speaker of the poem begins speaking because he can't reconcile the feeling he has that the world is "immeasurably alive and good" with what he sees around him as a dissolving, barren world. All sense of "home" is destroyed: the gray nest of the first stanza is "blown to a swirl"; the apple trees are bare of fruit; the house of stanza two is bare; the rooms are gray hollows; the windows are opaque; the air is deadened. The hills of stanza three are chewed away and the rabbits one would expect to find there are reduced to "bonehouses"—not houses at all, but dissolving skeletons; even the twilight is predatory and the stars' nest is no nest at all, but an object put on a shelf too high to be reached. The first three stanzas are about endings—the world rendered bare, a wasteland. The landscape recalls the "dark, wind-clawed trees," "moldering corpses," "small bones of rose," "odor of rotten apples," of "Vision and Elegy."

"The Quest" is a solid tetrameter four-stanza construction of end-stopped stanzas of one or two sentences each. The envelope rhyme scheme is similar to the scheme (ABBA CDDC) Rilke often used, but here Wright manages it much more skillfully than it was in the translations and adaptations. The poem begins in the past tense with the speaker as the survivor who has returned to a post-catastrophic world. It produces, by stanza four, a present in which a "you" is sought (Rilke would have understood this "you" as God or the beloved, or more likely both). The "I" seeks integration ("to know the world") that can only be supplied by an other. Yet the poem's final line, "Though bare as rifted paradise," collapses back on the deadened winter world that can be glimpsed (like a vision of the Grail) through the work being done by the poems, but can never be a permanent state. The paradise remains undermined, like the landscape along the Ohio River by the mining process that leaves the area both below and above unstable—so it both opens and ruins at the same time.

The "rifted paradise" of "The Quest" looks forward to the "vacant paradise" of "A Fit Against the Country," the first poem in *The Green Wall* and beyond to the dark Orpheus and Eurydice–like scene played out in "To the Muse," of *Shall We Gather at the River*, more fully examined in the following section.

Heine: Gladden My Heart

German voices sounded and resounded in Wright's work, whether as early poetry "rehearsals" or published translations, as adaptations and epigraphs from first to last. He used the phrase "Solitary Apprenticeships" for a group of German and Spanish translations he considered including in his 1962 manuscript "Now I Am Awakened," a precursor to *The Branch Will Not Break*. "Now I Am Awakened" (Nû bin ich erwachet) echoes a phrase from a Walther von der Vogelweide poem, "Alas! Where have all the years gone?"

On a handwritten table of contents for "Now I Am Awakened," Wright typed this note to himself:

Nov. 21, 62: Add to the new ms. The ff. (type it all out):

Solitary Apprenticeships

1. Anacreon's Grave (Goethe)
2. I Want to Sleep (J. Guillén)
3. De Profundis (Trakl)
4. Our Daily Bread (Vallejo)
5. Christ's Descent into Hell (Rilke)[13]

The Rilke translation, one of his best, was made with poet Sarah Youngblood (1927–1980), Wright's colleague at the University of Minnesota.

The "temporary" addition of five translations in an early version of *The Branch Will Not Break* reveals the extent to which Wright depended upon translation to maintain his poetic momentum and the vital place it had in his work well beyond his Kenyon years. It is interesting to note that on this short list the German translations outnumber the Spanish at a time when most critics believe that Spanish was the more significant influence on Wright's work. Ultimately, he did not include any of these poems in *The Branch Will Not Break*, but nearly ten years later, all, except for the Rilke, appear in *Collected Poems*, and *The Branch Will Not Break* has its German touchstones in epigraphs from Heine and Storm, and the translation, "Three Stanzas from Goethe."

The number of translations of the poems of Heinrich Heine (1797–1856) among Wright's Kenyon papers confirms that Heine was one of his major German interests. He was familiar with Heine's poems as early as the spring of 1950, his junior year at Kenyon. Wright's fascination with Heine grew into a passion as he listened to the extensive *lieder* collection of 78s available on campus. As he had with Rilke, he again followed his ear to Heine's poems, especially those set to music. "The sounds go on, and on, / In spite of what the morning / Or evening dark has done," he went on to write in *The Green Wall* in his "Poem for Kathleen Ferrier," the English contralto who sang on many of those 78s.

Heine was the favorite poet of German composers with nearly five thousand musical settings of his poems by Schubert, Schumann, Hugo Wolf, Liszt, Mendelssohn, Brahms, and many others. Drafts among the Kenyon papers show that Wright was reading widely in Heine's work and responding with his own translations and parodies. He wrote to John Furniss about his pleasure in Heine's *Book of Songs*: "Speaking of simplicity and grace, he is one of poetry's chief exponents of these virtues. He's very witty, too—but always tender."[14]

Wright's enthusiasm for *lieder* led him to translate nearly twenty of the short lyrics in Heine's best-known work, *Book of Songs* (1827). He published a collage of some of these poems in the Winter 1951 issue of *Hika*, the Kenyon literary magazine, under the title "Kleider machen Lause: ein Liederkranz" (Clothes Make the Man: A Song-cycle); Some Imitations of Heinrich Heine's German." (Note: The complete text of "Clothes Make the Man" is included in the "Selected German Translations" section of this book.)

Wright pulled these four imitations together under his own title, which is a mistranslation. "Kleider machen Lause" means "Clothes Make Louts," not "Clothes Make the Man." If there were an umlaut over the "a" in Lause, which either Wright or the editors of *Hika* failed to insert, the phrase would mean "Clothes Make Lice." It is possible that Wright was intentionally playing with the phrase since he is thoroughly enjoying himself in these imitations, playful versions that depart freely from Heine's poems, as did his Rilke imitations. At times, Wright parodies Heine's biting style with his own verses— Part IV of this "translation" is Wright's own invention, imitating Heine's style:

IV. INTRIGUE

Past ruin'd Ilion Helen lies,
Heroic wars are finished;
The gods have, in a various guise,
Appreciably diminished.

There is no Hero, by the way,
To watch Leander drown.
We literate lovers of today
Snivel, and write it down.

This writing takes the edges off
The old barbaric passion:
We wish we bellowed loud of love
In ancient singers' fashion.

Dearly beloved little heart,
Helen let Paris rape her.
We cannot take the true love's part
Unless we banish paper.[15]

At the University of Washington, in the spring of 1954, Wright made his most direct statement on what he'd learned from Heine in a workbook he presented to Theodore Roethke as part of a graduate writing course:

I have read Heine's poems a hundred times, memorized a great many of them, and studied his prose writings widely. I think he is not only very funny, but a great technician. As I say, he knows how to get to the point . . . I never try to write anything without bringing to bear on my own efforts Heine's speed, ruthless excision of ornaments, directness, and humor. I haven't succeeded in learning much of these yet, but that isn't Heine's fault. He is still right.[16]

More than ten years later, to mark the important inheritance of this excision of ornament, this directness and humor in the poems he was writing, Wright would place the final two stanzas from "Aus alten Märchen winkt es" ("From an old tale it beckons") untranslated on the title page of *The Branch Will Not Break*. This is the whole poem, which is well known as Song 15 of Robert Schumann's lovely song-cycle, *Dichterliebe*, Op. 48, in my own translation:

From an old tale it beckons
Forth with a white hand,
There's singing and ringing
Of a magic land:

Where enormous flowers languish
In golden afternoon light,
And tenderly gaze at each other
With bridal faces;—

Where all the trees speak
And sing like a choir,
And rushing springs gush forth
Like dance music;—

And love songs resound,
Like you have never heard,
Until a marvelously sweet longing
Bewitches you miraculously!

Ah, if I could go there,
And there gladden my heart,
And be relieved of all torment,
And be free and blessed.

Ah, that land of bliss!
I see it often in my dreams.
Yet comes the morning sun,
It dissolves like mere foam.

Well before its appearance with the poems of *The Branch Will Not Break*, Wright employed a dreamscape, Zauberland-like imagery of transformation, metamorphosis, and dissolution in the early poems of *The Green Wall* and *Saint Judas*. These are poems in which the human voice, that is the human spirit, is lost, or constrained, but takes nonhuman shape in order to become free:

from "The Quail" ll. 1–6

Lost in the brush, bound by the other path
To find the house,
You let me know how many voices,
How many shifting bodies you possessed,
How you could flit away to follow birds,
And yet be near.

from "Morning Hymn to a Dark Girl" ll. 39–44

You greet the river with a song so low
No lover on a boat can hear, you slide
Silkily to the water, where you rinse
Your fluted body, fearless; though alive
Orangutans, sway from the leaves and gaze,
Crocodiles doze along the oozy shore.

from "The Assignation" ll. 9–16

Inside the moon's hollow is a hale gray man
Who washed his hands, and waved me where to go:
Up the long hill, the mound of lunar snow,
Around three lapping pebbles, over the crossed
Arms of an owl nailed to the southern sky.
I spun three times about, I scattered high,
Over my shoulder, clouds of salt and dust.
The earth began to clear. I saw a man.

from "A Little Girl on Her Way to School" ll. 9–16

One bell before I woke, the stones
Under the balls of her soft feet
Cried out to her, the leaves in the wet
All tumbled toward her name at once,

And while my waking hung in poise
Between the air and the damp earth,
I saw her startle to the breath
Of birds beginning in her voice.

from "Evening" ll. 17–24

Then, struck beyond belief
By the child's voice I heard,
I saw his hair turn leaf,
His dancing toes divide
To hooves on either side,
One hand become a bird.
Startled, I held my tongue
To hear what note he sang.

from "Sparrows in a Hillside Drift" ll. 23–24, 28

I lose their words, though winter understands
Man is the listener gone deaf and blind.

. . .

A chimney whispers to a cloud of snow.

For the speaker of many of Wright's poems and in many of the
poems in Heine's *Buch der Lieder* (from which Wright's first Heine
translations were made), the threat to the human spirit is thwarted
or withheld love. The mood is overwhelmingly subjunctive: If only,
if only. Happiness is just out of reach, a fair season is just on the
edge of collapse, a love maddeningly here and gone. The burden of
the speaker in Heine is often to imagine a place, to sing a place into
being, where the lovers can be free:

On wings of song, my sweetheart,
I shall carry you away,
Away to the meadows by the Ganges,
I know the loveliest place there.[17]

*"Auf Flügeln des Gesanges" ll. 1–4,
translated by Peter Branscombe*

All the tenderness that Wright found in Heine is here in this poem
from *Lyrisches Intermezzo*. And Wright is often one of our tenderest
poets, too:

from "The Assignation," in *The Green Wall*

You sat beside the bed, you took my hands;
And when I lay beyond all speech, you said,
You swore to love me after I was dead,
To meet me in a grove and love me still,
Love the white air, the shadow where it lay.
Dear Love, I called your name in air today,
I saw the picnic vanish down the hill.
And waved the moon awake, with empty hands.

from "Moon," in *New Poems*

Come down to me love and bring me
One panther of silver and one happy
Evening of snow,
And I will give you
My life, my own, and now . . .

White shadow of cities where the scars
Of forgotten swans
Waken into feathers
And new leaves.

from "Speak," in *Shall We Gather at the River*

To speak in a flat voice
Is all that I can do.
I have gone every place
Asking for you.
Wondering where to turn
And how the search would end
And the last streetlight spin
Above me blind.

But Wright is not merely a dreamer, or an escape artist. His speakers often have the hard conviction of the cheated and the dark wisdom of Old Testament prophets. He "knows the world," with the speaker of "The Quest," as "immeasurably alive and good, / Though bare as rifted paradise"; he knows "that vacant paradise" behind the green wall; he finds that "though love can be a scarcely imaginable Hell, / By God, it is not a lie." (From "The Art of the Fugue: A Prayer," in *Two Citizens*.)

As we saw with several of the Rilke translations, a number of poems that Wright chose to translate from Heine deal with lost love. In Heine, too, Wright was drawn to poems about lovers separated by death, poems that echo the Orpheus-Eurydice theme. Heine's "Seegespenst" ("Sea Ghost"), for instance, tells the story of a sailor who gazes down into the water and sees the face of his drowned beloved. Here are Wright's last stanzas of his translation of "Seegespenst":

> While I, with my soul full of grief,
> Sought you across the whole earth,
> And sought you always,
> You always beloved
> Lost for so long,
> Finally found—
> I have found you and gaze again
> Into your sweet face,
>
> . . .
>
> And never will I lose you again,
> And I shall come down to you,
> And with outspread arms
> Crush you to my heart—[18]
>
> *James Wright translation*

In this water poem of Heine's *Die Nordsee* series, it wouldn't be wrong to feel a link with the continuing presence of Wright's alluring and dangerous Ohio River. "I shall come down to you," "Und ich komme hinab zu dir," assures Heine's speaker, a phrase that acts as a makeshift compass for Wright's many poems addressed to a lost beloved over the course of many years. This mysterious, compound figure, whom Wright often addresses as the poet's muse and often calls Jenny, is the dedicatee of *Shall We Gather at the River*. In fact, Heine's poem "An Jenny" ("To Jenny") in *Neue Gedichte* may be one source among several for Wright's idea for the name.

The final poem in *Shall We Gather at the River* is the disturbing "To the Muse," the first of Wright's Jenny poems.

> I would lie to you
> If I could.
> But the only way I can get you to come up
> Out of the suckhole, the south face

Of the Powhatan pit, is to tell you
What you know:

You come up after dark, you poise alone
With me on the shore.
I lead you back to this world. [ll. 11–19]

The world has tried to bury me, he says, down the Powhatan pit, the
way it has so many others in my Ohio, but through you, Jenny, maybe
I can get back up and out. Making poems is both the way down and
maybe the way out. The poem, as with so many of Wright's poems,
seems to be about the restoration of wholeness, the desire for the
defeat of loneliness and estrangement, an end to loss. It's as if he's
saying: Nothing short of the complete triumph of beauty, of para-
dise, will do for me. I will try anything, endure anything, to make
that happen.

This singing will require everything he has, then, echoing the line
of Rilke's so critical to him: "Es wird mein Leben sein" ("It will be
my life"). To illustrate, in "To the Muse," he gives us a nightmarish
scene of an after-hours clinic presided over by the Fates, or "Mac-
beth's" weird sisters, but more usefully it might be read as a metaphor
describing a contraption for speaking of the nearly unbearable pain
and strangeness of making poems:

Three lady doctors in Wheeling open
Their offices at night.
I don't have to call them, they are always there.
But they only have to put the knife once
Under your breast.
Then they hang their contraption.
And you bear it.

It's awkward a while. Still, it lets you
Walk about on tiptoe if you don't
Jiggle the needle.
It might stab your heart, you see.

The blade hangs in your lung and the tube
Keeps it draining.
That way they only have to stab you
Once. Oh Jenny. [ll. 20–34]

Making poems is so often like walking on tiptoe through love and
memory and childhood, careful not to jiggle the needle too much.
Otherwise, the poem will overwhelm your heart, as it drains the
poison off—for the recovery of self that only the poem can manage.
The beloved cannot be rescued in the end. "How can I live without
you?" the speaker in "To the Muse" ends, echoing Milton's Adam in
Book 9 of *Paradise Lost*, line 908. Adam says just this to Eve when he
discovers she has eaten the forbidden fruit. It is already too late for
her to "come up" to him. He takes the fruit himself, in order to die
with her. This speaker says:

How can I live without you?
Come up to me, love,
Out of the river, or I will
Come down to you. [ll. 45–48]

The line "Come up (or down) to me," encountered so long ago in
Heine, is spoken again and again throughout Wright's work when his
speakers are at their most haunted, most lonely, and most despairing:

from "A Prayer in My Sickness," in *Saint Judas*

Spinning in such bewildered sleep, I need
To know you, whirring above me, when I wake.
Come down. Come down. I lie afraid.
I have lain alien in my life so long.
How can I understand love's angry tongue?

from "Moon," in *New Poems*

Come down to me love and bring me
One panther of silver and one happy
Evening of snow

from "The Idea of the Good," in *New Poems*

I dream of my poor Judas walking along and alone
And alone and alone and alone till his wound
Woke and his bowels
Broke.
Jenny, I gave you that unhappy
Book that nobody knows but you.

from "Son of Judas," in *Two Citizens*

I'm getting out, this time.
Out of that body I prayed to get out of,
Out of that soul that only existed
In the Jenny sycamore that is now the one wing,
The only wing.

from "October Ghosts," in *Two Citizens*

Jenny cold, Jenny darkness,
They are coming back again.
We came so early,
But now we are shoveled down
The long slide.
We carry a blackened crocus
In either hand.

Friends, I have stolen this line from Robinson,
From Jenny, and from springtime, and from bone,
And from the quick nuthatch, the blooming of wing upon the
    sky.
Now I know nothing, I can die alone.

With Wright we feel the ghost of Heine drifting alongside that of Rilke at the edges of his poems, applying pressure here and there, leaving a trace, or sounding a note. Even though he never published a translation of either after college, the undersong of their voices is everywhere in his work.

While more than half of the drafts of translations from Wright's early undergraduate years come from the poetry of Rilke, Heine, and Storm, there are at least thirteen additional German poets represented among his papers. Among these are translations of poems by Walther von der Vogelweide (ca. 1170–1230) and several anonymous minnesingers. Vogelweide is the best known of the German singers of love, who, like the troubadours of other countries, wandered from court to court in medieval Europe. He was the first minnesinger to break the code of courtly love by writing songs not only to "courtly" ladies, but also to women of "lower birth," and occasionally defied convention by writing of requited love, as in his best-known lyric "Unter der Linden."

An uncollected poem of the 1950s, "To a Visitor from My Home Town," is another of Wright's many adaptations, like those of the Rilke and Heine poems, part translation, part original poem. This one is a version of Vogelweide's poem, "Weh Mir, O Jahr":

TO A VISITOR FROM MY HOME TOWN

(an imitation of Walther von der Vogelweide)

I spend so often calling out
Of darkness what I know:
The ugly town I wept about
In winter long ago;
The sooty color of all tears,
The jerk of crippled trees,
And leaves grown rotten as the years
Began to eat the grass.

One summer when a friend of mine
Drowned at the river's edge,
The local diver dropped a line
After the hook and dredge;
The diver and the grappling hook
Raised to the skiff and shore—

I cannot write down in a book
What child the water bore.

I cannot trick out lightly now
The children of that town.
I shut my eyes and cannot know
Whether the trees are down,
Whether the railroad trestle falls
In shadow on the place
Where the drunk hoboes lay by walls
And hid the human face.

Yet I remember poplar boughs
Twist in their dying leaves;
Two brothers, welcome at my house,
Have grown up to be thieves.
Now I have broken out like one
More criminal still than they:
And the freedom of my flesh and bone
Is what I steal today.[19]

Here is the first stanza of Vogelweide's fifty-one-line poem:

Alas! Where have all the years gone?
Did I dream my life, or is it real?
What I always thought—was that something?
Then I've slept and don't know it . . .
Now I'm awake, and I no longer know
What used to be familiar as my own hands:
People and places, where I was raised from childhood,
They are strangers to me, as if it were all lies.
Those who were my playmates are old and indolent.
Meadows are farmed, forests are felled,
If it were not for the water, which flows as ever before,
Ah, then I'd believe that my misfortune is truly great.
Many no longer even greet me, who once knew me well.

The world is full of ingratitude everywhere.
When I think of the many glorious days,
They disappear, like ripples in the water—
Forever more—alas![20]

This Vogelweide poem, one of many Wright translated or adapted at the same time he was writing the poems that became *The Green Wall* and *Saint Judas*, is one clear artistic source of his critically noted "complicated" Ohio valley poems. This imitation is stylistically situated between his Rilke imitation "Vision and Elegy" and the first poem in *The Green Wall*, "A Fit Against the Country."

Wright published "To a Visitor" in the Winter/Spring 1957 issue of *Assay*, the literary magazine of the English department at the University of Washington—an issue dedicated to Wright, who "was leaving the University this year to take up his duties as an Instructor of English at the University of Minnesota." Four Wright poems are in this issue, and all four relate to his childhood in Martins Ferry. One of these poems, "An Offering for Mr. Bluehart," appears exactly as it does in *Saint Judas* (1959), and these four poems contain the seeds of many of Wright's later themes: drowned children, the diver (John Shunk) who brought up their bodies, drunken hoboes, thieves, and Wright's "escape" from the Ohio Valley. Wright's interest in the German poets often leads Wright back to his childhood in Martins Ferry and the poems of Vogelweide seem to do so more directly than any others.

In an interview that appeared in the *American Poetry Review* 9, no. 3 (1980), the poet Dave Smith asked Wright, what might a sense of place mean to a writer? In the course of a lengthy reply, Wright talks about the Ohio Valley where he grew up:

My feeling about the Ohio Valley is, again, complicated. I sometimes feel a certain nostalgia about the place. At the same time I realize that as my friend Tom Hodge, now a surgeon in California, wrote to me a few years ago our problem when we were boys in Martins Ferry, Ohio, in the industrial area enclosed by the foothills of the Appalachians on both sides, near that big river, was to get out.[21]

This imitation looks back to the imagery of "Vision and Elegy": the rotting leaves, the crippled trees, the soot-colored tears. When the speaker of "To a Visitor" ends by asserting: "Now I have broken out . . ." and "the freedom of my flesh and bone / Is what I steal today," Wright is looking forward to the exhortation in the final stanza of "Fit Against the Country":

Yet, body, hold your humor
Away from the tempting tree,
The grass, the luring summer
That summon the flesh to fall.
Be glad of the green wall
You climbed across one day,
When winter stung with ice
That vacant paradise.

And he looks back to the Vogelweide poem itself in which the speaker asks:

Alas! Where have all the years gone?
Did I dream my life, or is it real?
What I always thought . . . was that something?
Then I've slept and don't know it . . .
Now I am awake, and no longer know
What used to be familiar as my own hands:

There we see that phrase: *Now I am awakened*—Vogelweide's *Nû Bin Ich Erwachet*—a version of the line Wright will choose as one of his working titles for *The Branch Will Not Break*. He often reused lines from his adaptations in his own poems, especially this line, leading to considerable confusion about which Vogelweide poem he was working on at which time. But a handwritten table of contents

"All men are not worthy of love." — Freud

Self-pity at the
Murderer's Grave
to J. L. D.

Pellets of lime show lightly through the grass.
My name is James A. Wright, and I was born
Twenty-five miles ~~from here~~ from here, in the same dirt.
~~His buried killer~~ lies no friend of mine,
His hands are claws to me, his moron's face
a snuffing slag-heap. All Ohio 'haint
Is the dead killer's ~~haunt~~, and that is to say
I have no pity for ~~the~~ bastard, now
Or any other time. Dying's the best
Of all the arts men learn in a dead place.
I walked here once. I made a loud display,
Leaning for language on a dead man's voice.
~~and now~~ Only they dying fills my mind today,
And so I add my sound to the rest.

Doty, if I confess I do not love you,
Will you let me alone?
The nights electrocute my fugitive,
My mind, that was like the ~~that~~ bewildered ~~mob~~
Yanked into dark, muttering self-lullabies.
Now it is dusk, I cannot lift my eyes.
My shadow flees me over wattacked stone.

~~I pity myself because a man is dead.~~
Imbecile, he demanded love from girls,
And murdered one. Also, he was a thief.
He left two women, and the last with child.
The base, foul as a dog's upon his head,
Made such revolting Ohio animals
Fitter for prayer than for an honest grief.
I have ~~but~~ no pity for the dead that starve,
And no love's lost between me and the crying
Drunks of Bellaire, Ohio. Let them shrink,
Die, in them own good time, for all of me.
Alive and dead, those sons of bitches who
Can do without my ~~witness~~ thirty years ago
Over the dead with paid twenty. ~~widely painted sighing~~
I do not pity the dead, I pity the dying,
I pity myself because a man is dead.

2.2 An early draft of Wright's second George Doty poem, "At the Executed Murderer's Grave," first published in 1958 in *Poetry*. Much changed, the poem appeared in *Saint Judas*.

among his papers dated June 19, 1958, shows that Wright intended to include "Weh Mir, O Jahr" ("Alas, O Year") first in *Saint Judas* (1959) and later in a revised form in *The Branch Will Not Break* (1963). His attraction to the poems of Vogelweide ran deep and continued far beyond his discovery of the poet at Kenyon.

The speaker in "To a Visitor" is the speaker of many Wright poems about Martins Ferry over the years—a generous, sympathetic speaker who doesn't want to look, but can't look away either. This is an attitude of critical importance to Wright's work in general that holds—almost impossibly—the urgencies of both inner and outer world in mind at the same time. He feels like an outsider but doesn't want to treat his hometown simply as a subject, looking at it as if he were not in it, too. He feels he has to steal his freedom—even this inalienable right, basic as his own flesh and bone—and confesses to being more than criminal, for wanting to escape.

Some of his most powerful and best-known poems—"Autumn Begins in Martins Ferry, Ohio," "At the Executed Murderer's Grave," "In Response to a Rumor that the Oldest Whorehouse in Wheeling, West Virginia, Has Been Condemned"—take up the complicated relationship with home. This voice in all its directness and evasion, all its tenderness and rage, is both the means of escape and the path of imaginative return.

from "At the Executed Murderer's Grave," in *Saint Judas*

My name is James A. Wright, and I was born
Twenty-five miles from this infected grave,
In Martins Ferry, Ohio, where one slave
To Hazel-Atlas Glass became my father.
He tried to teach me kindness. I return
Only in memory now, aloof, unhurried,
To dead Ohio, where I might lie buried,
Had I not run away before my time.
Ohio caught George Doty. Clean as lime,
His skull rots empty here. Dying's the best
Of all the arts men learn in a dead place.

I walked here once. I made my loud display,
Leaning for language on a dead man's voice.
Now sick of lies, I turn to face the past.
I add my easy grievance to the rest:

Theodor Storm: To Get Home

Years before he chose lines from *Frauen-Ritornelle* by Theodor Storm
as an epigraph for his "Goodbye to the Poetry of Calcium," a key
poem in *The Branch Will Not Break*, Wright dove deeply into Storm's
work at Kenyon. Later he received a Fulbright scholarship to Vienna
to study Storm more fully. What he found in Storm's poems and
stories over the years, he writes, was that:

> ... the chance to work on the Storm translation was, more than
> once, the chance to go on living, almost the one chance ...
> Never once was it a burden. It was always, rather, a source of
> nourishment and refreshment; and the completion of the book
> is the fulfillment of an old dream of mine.
>
> It is spring, and ... the leaves are
> falling upward![22]

Translations of fourteen Storm poems are among the papers from
Wright's college days. In the fall of 1951, he published "Elegiac Verses
for Theodor Storm," similar to his Rilke elegy and in which Storm
becomes another ghostly guide. Here are the first two stanzas (with
an epigraph from Storm):

> *O Stimme des Tages, mein Herz ist Bang*
> (O voice of the day, my heart is fearful)
>
> The day is gone already, and the night
>   Is on the Warnock forest dark and bare,
>
> As on the Frisian dunes, whereover [sic] flight
>   Of mews moils up the air,

Where down again into the waters go
　　The gulls; and upward from the waves again

Their voices and their wings in evening grow
　　Inevitably as human pain.[23]

Like his poem for Rilke, "Vision and Elegy," the Storm poem is set in rural Warnock, Ohio, and Wright inserts several phrases and images from Storm's stories: "the dikes have crumbled" (from "Der Schimmelreiter"), the "floating lilies" (from "Immensee"), and "children drowned" (from "Aquis Submersus"). These appropriations, like the earlier ones from Rilke, show he was reading and taking in Storm's stories early on. Again, the sense of loss, and the inability to keep the image of the beloved against its vanishing, echoes in these lines from the Storm elegy:

　　　　　It is the face of the beloved fades
　　Into the clean austerity of air.

Wright is struck in Storm's work by that sense of longing he found in Rilke's Orpheus/Eurydice story and those of the drowned or lost lover in Heine's poems.

Several of the Storm stories he was then reading and translating were published as *The Rider on the White Horse* by E. L. Doctorow, a Kenyon classmate, when he was an editor at New American Library. Wright contributed a short foreword to the 1964 volume in which he praises these late stories of Storm in terms that might have been a description of the struggles he was facing with his own art at the time:

> . . . the very last of his works, shows how far beyond those conventions his own artistic imagination eventually forced him to reach. By the time he came to write *The Rider on the White Horse*, Storm had resolved the unavoidable conflict between his own personal imaginative impulse and the constricting literary conventions within which he had learned his art.[24]

A glance at a list of Wright's published works reveals his interest in the German novelist and poet Hermann Hesse, and by publishing two volumes of Hesse translations, *Poems* (1970) and *Wandering: Notes and Sketches by Hermann Hesse* (1972), Wright offered more single editions of Hesse's work than of any other German poet. In the Translator's Note to Hesse's *Poems*, he states: "All I wish to do is to offer a selection of Hesse's poems which deal with the single theme of homesickness."[25] Later in that introduction, he quoted a passage from the closing pages of Hesse's novel *Steppenwolf*, a passage he tells the reader he used as a guide in selecting and translating these poems. The passage ends with Hesse's character Hermine talking to Harry Haller:

> Ah, Harry, we have to stumble through so much dirt and humbug before we reach home. And we have no one to guide us. Our only guide is our homesickness.[26]

Wright explains further: "That is what I think Hesse's poetry is about. He is homesick. But what is home? I do not know the answer, but I cherish Hesse because he at least knew how to ask the question." These observations on Hesse are strikingly similar to those Wright made in his introductory remarks to his earlier translations of Storm's stories. As he noted in the foreword to *The Rider on the White Horse*: ". . . the main thing is not to get on in the world but to get home."[27] "Heimweh" (homesickness) is a major theme in the two German poets Wright published in major collections.

Although the Hesse translations appear in 1970 and 1972, Wright's interest in Hesse, like the other German poets he translated (except for Trakl), dates back to his undergraduate years at Kenyon. Among drafts from Wright's Kenyon years were six translations from Hesse, and the published versions are similar to those early versions.

Wanderung (*Wandering*), published by Hesse in 1920, is a collection of prose passages, poems, and watercolor sketches by Hesse. Wright's and his teenage son Franz's translations, published fifty-two years later, mark the first time Hesse's book appeared in English. On the back cover of the volume, the Farrar, Straus and Giroux editors noted:

> On May 2, 1919, Hesse wrote to Romain Rolland: "I have had to bear a very heavy burden in my personal life in recent years. Now I am about to go to Ticino once again, to live for a while as a hermit in nature and in my work."[28]

In a letter to Helen McNeely Sheriff shortly after he and Franz finished their work on *Wandering*, Wright describes the book to her as "a strange and haunting work, a kind of metaphysical travel-book."[29] Hesse begins with a sad farewell to his home and life in Germany, and the book develops into a meditation on longing, memory, and nature as Hesse discovers the way to a new and hopeful life. The book confronts homesickness and transforms it. In "The Farmhouse," the first prose passage in the book, Hesse speaks of his sense of "Heimweh": "I want to taste my homesickness, as I taste my joy."[30] This volume also highlights Wright's growing interest in Hesse's prose passages and validates them as a poetic form. Wright called these prose passages "prose pieces," the term he preferred in his own work. In the later years of his career, prose pieces became an important part of Wright's own volumes, and his translation of *Wanderung* played a significant role in his own exploration of the prose poem as a form.

In her prefatory remarks on the editing of *Above the River: The Complete Poems of James Wright* (1990) Anne Wright notes:

> After *Two Citizens*, James began to work on prose pieces and published a series of them in the 1976 chapbook *Moments of the Italian Summer*. Seven of these pieces appear in revised form in *To a Blossoming Pear Tree*. Another group of prose pieces, written in 1979, came out in *The Summers of James and Annie Wright* (1981). These two chapbooks were combined in the later publication *The Shape of the Light*. The prose pieces in *Above the River* are placed after *Two Citizens*, the point in his career when he first wrote in this form.[31]

Two Citizens was published in 1973, one year after Wright and his son translated *Wanderung*, and his prose poems began to appear shortly thereafter.

Wright's *Moments of the Italian Summer* (1976), a volume which contains only prose poems, is a work much like Hesse's *Wanderung* and is a wonderful example of a German poet's influence on Wright's own work. *Moments* contains fourteen prose pieces and six drawings by Joan Root. Wright's hand is evident in the conception of the chapbook, including the idea of using illustrations, which makes the book even more like Hesse's *Wanderung*. Set in Italy as is Wright's *Moments*, both books were curative works for the poets, written during periods when they sought refuge from their everyday lives and locales, with time to "wander" and take in light, nature, and love—reminiscent of Goethe's and Heine's journeys into the Harz mountains. The first prose piece in *Moments*, "The Secret of Light," ends like this and Wright's "precious secret" becomes an "open secret":

> It is all right with me to know that my life is only one life. I
>   feel like the light of the river Adige.
> By this time, we are both an open secret. (Verona)[32]

Hesse's poems influenced the tone of Wright's later poetry, which becomes softer and more tranquil. It is almost as if Wright comes full circle in many of his later poems, returning to the delicate lyricism of Asia he had discovered when he was stationed in Japan, 1946–47, and which he continued to admire in the Chinese poets, especially of the T'ang Dynasty. Rediscovering Hesse in the early 1970s led Wright down a contemplative road, most often toward simplicity, clarity, and renewal. In the first prose passage Wright translated in *Wanderung*, Hesse affirms: "The way to salvation leads neither to the left nor the right: it leads into your own heart, and there alone is God, and there alone is peace."[33]

No German poet transformed Wright's poetry the way Georg Trakl did. Rilke, Heine, Storm, Goethe, Hesse, and the other German poets he encountered at Kenyon had their effect on him, but it was his reading and translation of Trakl that wrought the greatest changes in his own work. Trakl touched a deep and dark nerve, a kind of madness and energy that simmered for six years until Wright met Robert Bly. Working with Bly at the farm's kitchen table on the Trakl translations gave Wright the courage to leave his safe traditional poetic forms behind, to go deeper into his self, to change his life.

> *from* "Lying in a Hammock at William Duffy's Farm
>   in Pine Island, Minnesota"
>
> Over my head, I see the bronze butterfly,
> Asleep on the black trunk,
> Blowing like a leaf in green shadow.
> Down the ravine behind the empty house,
> The cowbells follow one another
> Into the distances of the afternoon.

When Wright "wandered" into the dimly lit classroom at the University of Vienna in 1952 and heard Professor Eugene Susini reading Trakl's "Verfall" (Decline), the stage had been set for him to receive Trakl's radical "new" poetry, an encounter that would eventually bring a sea change in his own work. "Verfall," a sonnet, is the first poem in Georg Trakl's *Die Dichtungen*, the three-volume edition from which Susini read Trakl's poems to the class. Ironically, Trakl's poetry, which was responsible, in part, for the "freeing" of his poetic line, first came to him in the form of a sonnet, a form Wright cherished. His intense apprenticeship to German poetry at Kenyon prepared him to be moved and energized by Trakl's powerful images and sudden associations. As he recounted nearly ten years later in the introduction to *Twenty Poems of Georg Trakl* (1961): "It was as though the sea had entered the class at the last moment. For this poem was not like any poem I had ever recognized." In that same introduction,

Wright summarizes why Trakl's work was so revolutionary and why it meant so much to him:

> We are used to reading poems whose rules of traditional construction we can memorize and quickly apply. Trakl's poems, on the other hand, though they are shaped with the most beautiful delicacy and care, are molded from within. He did not write according to any "rules of construction" traditional or other, but rather waited patiently and silently for the worlds of his poems to reveal their own natural laws. The result, in my experience at least, is a poetry from which all shrillness and clutter have been banished . . . His poems are not objects to be used and then cast aside, but entrances into places where deep, silent labors go on.[34]

By the time Wright wrote these words, Trakl's influence had been unleashed in his own work, but the road to that transformation had been a long one. Wright had gone to Kenyon because John Crowe Ransom was there, and he wanted to learn the craft of poetry. He loved the discipline of Ransom's poetry, its self-containment and its form, and he loved Ransom, so his decision to turn to "free" verse was not an easy one. After years of rigorous training in all aspects of prosody, Wright had paid in full for his freedom and was ready to take a "spiritual" leap into a new blossoming of poetry.

After graduating from Kenyon, Wright's love of German poetry took him to Vienna to study the poetry of Theodor Storm, and when he blundered into Susini's classroom, that accidental turning brought him to Trakl and set him on an unexpected path. Before the discovery of the many translations from German among his undergraduate papers, and the knowledge of his extensive studies in German language and literature at Kenyon, Trakl was perhaps the only German poet readers associated with Wright, save for the Goethe epigraph and translation in *The Branch Will Not Break*.

Despite Wright's attraction to Trakl's poetry, only three Trakl translations exist among his drafts from that year in Vienna: "Geburt" (Birth), "An die Verstummten" (To the Mute Ones), and "An einen Frühverstorbenen" (To One Early Dead). His first wife Liberty noted that during their stay in Vienna Wright spent much of his time reading and absorbing the cultural life of the city—the language, the music, the literature—and in writing his own poems.

He also met Herbert Lindenberger, a fellow Fulbright scholar, in Susini's class. Both men were immediately taken with the Austrian's poetry and became friends, discussing Trakl in the coffee houses. During their days together, Lindenberger had the opportunity to observe first-hand Wright's command of the German language:

> It was a good reading knowledge, and he was very sensitive to the sound of German poetry. It was never fluent in a spoken way. I think he got most of what Susini was saying . . . When we were together in Vienna I did nearly all the talking of German to the natives since I was raised bilingually so I rarely heard him try to speak. The important thing for him was that he could deal with the poetry.[35]

Lindenberger's comment that Wright was "very sensitive to the sound of German poetry" again validates the importance of the musical quality of German poetry that attracted Wright. Though most discussions of Trakl's influence on Wright focus on the importance of Trakl's images, which were certainly significant, it was their fusion with the sound of Trakl that drew him in.

Wright's time in Vienna marks the end of his lengthiest and most intense period of contact with the German language. During the years 1949–1953, Wright laid a foundation in German language and literature that remained solid throughout his life's work.

After his stay in Vienna, at the suggestion of Lindenberger, Wright entered graduate school at the University of Washington where he took a writing seminar with poet Theodore Roethke in the spring of 1954. Roethke required students to keep a workbook throughout the semester in which they were to study the metrics of a poet's lines and imitate them, as a way to tune their ears to verbal music.

Roethke's concern for the sound and rhythm of words was the

impetus behind the exercises he assigned his students and what he stressed in his own poetry. The workbook was to be revised, typed, and submitted as part of the final grade.

Wright's workbooks among the Roethke papers in the library of the University of Washington contain exercises in which he closely examines poems and lines from Trakl, including a special section he titled "Notes on the Metrics of the Austrian Poet Georg Trakl." This section on Trakl displays Wright's attention to Trakl's metrics, doing exactly what Roethke urged his students to do—to break down a poet's lines to discover how he or she made their music, something Wright had been attempting to do for some time. Wright's notes show that he gave Trakl's poems a thorough new critical reading, in which he dissected individual lines and studied the rhyme and meter in a way that Ransom would have applauded. This excerpt from the revised 1954 Workbook offers Wright's analysis of three lines from Trakl:

A Sample of an Exercise in Metrics and Sounds
      Schön ist der Mensch und erscheinen im Dunkel,
  Wenn er staunend Arme und Beine bewegt,
    Und in purpurnen Höhlen stille die Augen rollen . . .
    (Trakl, "Helian II")[36]

Below these lines, Wright discusses Trakl's meter in exacting detail. This excerpt from his first paragraph shows how rigorously he studied the metrics of the lines in an attempt to discover their secrets:

Here the first two lines are moved in one direction, anapaestically. The third line begins lightly with two anapaests. Suddenly, at "stille," come [sic] a dactyl and two trochees . . . This is metrical dissonance. It is highly, dramatically effective to me. It is a slight shift that belongs to the structure of human speech; to the developments of the breath; a slight gasp.[37]

Wright was mining Trakl's poems for his own creations, and he goes on to discuss how he plans to use what he had learned from Trakl by including a short poem he was working on:

Three or four poems or fragments have grown so far out of this search of mine. Here is the first one, almost an English transcription of the way of Trakl in his stony and glum little elegiac poems about symbolic landscapes:

IN A PARK

> Do you suffer still, gods in the stone?
> Coils ripple without rain in the bluish water.
> The thrush, laid at the feet of the evening,
> Glides, biered [sic] on a float of lily flakes.
> The corpse laments by drifting.
> So will I bow to the foreheads of granite Apollos,
> The scattered memory of marble.

Wright then comments with a critical eye on his Trakl imitation:

> This poem obviously does not work. It has no wholeness. It does not begin and end. The reason for its not working is important to me, and sends me back to a deliberate comparison of two lines, one out of Trakl, and the other out of [Louise] Bogan:
>
> > Deine Lippen trinken die Kühle des blauen Felsenquells.
> > . . . The summer thunder, like a wooden bell . . .
>
> Bogan's phrase, again, has the richer effect because it is spare, because she has learned what to leave out (how? how?). Because all her echoes are deployed around the faint difference in sound between "m" and "n" in the phrase "the summer thunder." Jesus God, how am I ever going to control myself?[38]

Another poem, "Soft Sonata," which grew out of this close study of Trakl, appears later in the 1954 Workbook and meant so much to Wright that he included it in an early manuscript of *The Green Wall.* The title "Soft Sonata" (sanfte Sonate) is taken from the second stanza of Trakl's long poem "Helian," which begins:

Abends auf der Terrasse betranken wir uns mit braunem Wein.
Rötlich glüht der Pfirsich im Laub;
Sanfte Sonate, frohes Lachen.

Evenings on the terrace we got drunk on brown wine
The peach glows red in the foliage;
Soft sonata, gay laughter.

translated by Saundra Rose Maley

Wright's "Soft Sonata" is, in fact, an imitation of "Helian," an important Trakl poem that Wright knew well. According to Lindenberger, the significance of "Helian" lies in the fact that the poem displays the "full flowering of Trakl's free-verse manner,"[39] which may have caused this poem to have a greater impact on Wright, since "Soft Sonata," his "Helian" imitation, is a much freer poem than most he was composing at the time. It is unrhymed and unmetered, but Wright was still reluctant to break entirely out of form and fuse his images and associations the way Trakl does and as he would do later in *The Branch Will Not Break*. A typed table of contents among Wright's papers for one early version of *The Green Wall*, "The Riches of the Air," includes five of the poems in the 1954 Workbook: "Soft Sonata," "Eleutheria," "Autumnal," "The Quail," and "The Quest." Of these five poems, only "Soft Sonata" and "The Quest" are not included ultimately in *The Green Wall*. "The Quest," a poem he wrote in Vienna, is a significant one in Wright's oeuvre, and he later reconsiders its importance and gives it a prominent position at the head of *Collected Poems* (1971).[40]

Wright's deep reading of "Helian," with its underlying Christian themes and images, may have contributed to the creation of the poem "Saint Judas." In his spiral notebook, an incomplete "imitation" from Trakl in German is followed by what may be the first handwritten version of "Saint Judas," showing Wright's marginal note and his changes in brackets, as he was shaping the poem into its final sonnet form. What is interesting about this transcription of a draft is that it comes on the heels of Wright's deep reading and re-examination of Trakl. The brackets are Wright's own, and we can see his notes on the left:

[Saint] Judas

When I went out to kill myself, I caught
A pack of hoodlums beating up a man.
Running to spare his suffering, I forgot
My name, my number, how the day began,
How soldiers milled around the garden stone
And sang amusing songs; how all that day
Their javelins measured crowds; how I alone

Clarify   Bargained the proper coins, and slipped away;
this   Banished from heaven,
phrase—   How I came here, to find this victim beaten,
probably   Stripped, kneed, and left to cry. Dropping my rope
stop//at   Aside, I ran, [forgot] ignored the uniforms:
end of   Then I remembered bread [my flesh] had eaten,
octave   The kiss that ate my [flesh]. Flayed without hope
           I held the man for nothing in my arms.[41]

Another poem, "To a Troubled Friend," in the 1954 Workbook under Roethke's assignment on "the 5-beat line," appears in *The Green Wall*. While Wright was working out complicated ideas about metrics and the line, he was writing many of the poems that would become his first book. Twenty-one of the forty-two poems in the "The Riches of the Air" and "Eleutheria" manuscripts appear in *The Green Wall*, chosen by W. H. Auden as the winner of the Yale Series of Younger Poets in 1956.

Theodore Roethke made this terminal comment in Wright's 1954 Workbook:

I think that Wright seemed kinda sunk this quarter too. I know he writes a scholarly line, but I think that he could afford to bend in the other direction for a while. This long piece, I don't know the name, has sparks of fire. He wrote it quite a while ago. Although it's messy, and factually at fault in spots, I think it shows that Jim Wright, a rugged but scholarly poet, has some opinions in common with myself about what makes poetry go.[42]

The return to Trakl's work in Roethke's class gave Wright an impetus toward change in his own poems. An entry in that 1954 Workbook reveals his growing definition of poetry—how the exercises with Trakl's lines, the metrics of the other poets he was reading, and Roethke's insistence on the importance of music in poetry were powerful forces in moving him further along his path. In another entry in that Workbook, Wright discusses an important shift in his beliefs about poetry:

> I have heretofore believed that the conceptual aspects of a poem should arbitrarily dictate to its substance; music could, and should, be sacrificed to meaning. I have now begun to realize that this is not so. I begin to realize the true intricacy and difficulty of Poetry. Neither meaning nor music can be "sacrificed."[43]

Appropriately, in the essay "The Work of James Wright" in *The Sixties* no. 8 (Spring 1966), Robert Bly was the first to discuss Trakl's influence on Wright[44]:

> Rereading Trakl gave him the hope that poetry in the next decade could be something more than verse. When he did return to poetry, the influence of Trakl brought in a new tone. The new tone did not mean an obvious correspondence between the two poetries. Rather, the poems begin to come from farther back in the brain. "In Fear of Harvests," for example, goes this way:
>
> > It has happened
> > Before: nearby,
> > The nostrils of slow horses
> > Breathe evenly,
> > And the brown bees drag their high garlands,
> > Heavily,
> > Toward hives of snow.[45]

Two pages later, Bly continues:

The poem most clearly influenced by Trakl is the poem called "Rain." Trakl has a confidence in the spiritual unity of the world. He therefore makes statements with qualification.

"Where the skulls are, God's eyes silently open." In Trakl a series of images makes a series of events. Because these events appear out of their "natural" order, without connectives we have learned to expect from reading newspapers, doors silently open into unused parts of the brain. Here is Wright's poem, "Rain":

It is the sinking of things.

Flashlights drift over dark trees,
Girls kneel,
An owl's eyelids fall.

The sad bones of my hands descend into a valley
Of strange rocks.[46]

Bly's discussion of "Rain" ends here, but his summation toward the end of the essay captures what he as the best-informed eyewitness saw Wright trying to do in his new poetry:

His lines are not stiff like sticks, but flexible like a living branch. Some emotion, rising very close to the surface, always seems to keep the words alive. In thought, his words, underneath are in touch with something infinite . . .
His work shows an unusual intellectual enthusiasm. Behind the pleasant sense of something new in language lies a conscious and deliberate rejection of an entire structure of thought, which is very well understood. Behind the subtle language, which seems all emotion and fragrance, lies intellectual energy, in this case, extremely powerful intellectual energy.[47]

Wright produced hundreds of German translations covering the work of sixteen poets during his undergraduate years at Kenyon (1948–1952), and again in the period shortly after he met Robert Bly and began working on the poems of *The Branch Will Not Break*

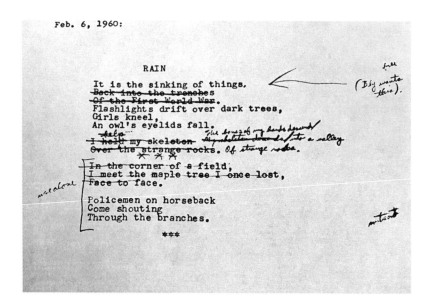

Feb. 6, 1960:

RAIN

It is the sinking of things.
~~Back into the trenches~~
~~Of the First World War.~~
Flashlights drift over dark trees,
Girls kneel,
An owl's eyelids fall.
~~help~~
~~I hold my skeleton~~
~~Over the strange rocks. Of strange rocks.~~

~~In the corner of a field,~~
~~I meet the maple tree I once lost,~~
~~Face to face.~~

Policemen on horseback
Come shouting
Through the branches.

***

2.3   A draft of "Rain" dated February 6, 1960, shows the evolution of the final two lines, the trimming of two stanzas, and the note "Bly wants this." Robert Bly called "Rain" the Wright poem "most clearly influenced by Trakl."

(1958–1963). During the first stage of immersion, Wright was engaged in an intensive apprenticeship to his craft, and his many German translations were a rigorous part of that discipline in rhyme and meter—the *music*—while presenting him with models for dealing with his philosophical questions concerning love, death, and nature. His second period of intense German translation coincides with a crucial transition in his creative and personal life—the years just before the publication of *Saint Judas* (1959) to the publication of the groundbreaking *The Branch Will Not Break* (1963). These two volumes stand like bookends, enclosing the years in which Wright moves from being a poet established in traditional forms to an innovator experimenting with free verse and radical new imagery. From his first encounter with Trakl's work in Vienna, through his close study and imitation of Trakl's metrics in the graduate seminar with Theodore Roethke, on through the translations with Bly, deep, silent labors were at work within him as he mined the German and Spanish poems for a new poetry. Wright was one of the first American poets to understand the importance of Trakl's poetry. He had an instinct, a "poetic intuition," that opened him up to new ideas and *forced* him to make associations.

In 1957 when Wright reluctantly left his beloved Seattle, the University of Washington, and Roethke for the University of Minnesota, where he would teach while finishing his dissertation, "The Comic Imagination of the Young Dickens," he was already recognized as a promising young poet. Though disappointed and feeling exiled, his move to Minneapolis placed him at the center of a new American poetry.

The summer afternoon of July 22, 1958, when Wright discovered Trakl's name on the back cover of a magazine called *The Fifties* that had found its way into his faculty mailbox is one of the most auspicious moments in the history of American poetry in the second half of the twentieth century. After reading the magazine several times, Wright immediately wrote the editor, Robert Bly, a "sixteen-page" letter. In that wonderful and agonized letter, he writes of his first exposure to Trakl's poetry six years earlier in Vienna:

> And every afternoon at 3 o'clock, I think it was four days a week,
> I walked through that terrible cold and unheated winter city,
> to hear Susini whisper in his beautiful, gentle, liquid voice the
> poems of an Austrian of whom I had never even heard, but who
> had the grasp and shape of what you in your article called the
> new imagination. I tried to catch it. I didn't understand how
> to *do* it . . . But back in America I have had an impossible time
> even trying to get anyone to admit that Whitman existed, to
> find anyone at all—anyone at all—who has even heard Trakl's
> name.[48]

In the letter, Wright describes writing his own despairing "farewell" to poetry:

> Plodding through the images of the slag heaps and the black
> trees and the stool-washed river and the chemicals from the
> factories of Wheeling Steel, Blaw Knox, the Hanna Coal Co.
> which . . . are the only images of childhood I can ever have, I

begged pardon . . . of the Mother of Roots or whoever the hell she is who gets into Whitman, Trakl, Neruda, Lorca, Char, Michaux—into almost everybody, in fact, except me. And I said—as obscurely and gibberingly as I *felt* like saying—that the hell with it, I was getting *out*. And I got out.[49]

Early the morning before he wrote this letter, Wright had written out one of the first of many drafts of "His Farewell to Poetry," which would become a signal poem in the "new style" placed right up front in *The Branch Will Not Break*.

And he didn't get out. That first issue of *The Fifties*, and Bly's insistence upon the central place the new imagination held in the work of the Spanish and German poets, saved Wright's creative life. With relief and gratitude, he confessed to Bly:

> I'm beginning to think, this evening, that I must have been really suffering with this sense of failure, of betraying what within me I genuinely *knew*, though I denied it on the surface, what poetry was . . . You've blasted open in me an abandoned cavern where the sacred mysteries used to be clumsily but reverently celebrated . . .[50]

Come out to the farm, Bly wrote, and Wright did. In Madison he explored the possibilities of the "new imagination," and it had been the Austrian poet, Georg Trakl, who brought them together. The very day Wright arrived at the farm, the two poets began translating Trakl. His "rediscovery" of Trakl, Rilke, Heine, Storm, and Goethe, and his coming to know the poems of César Vallejo, Juan Ramón Jiménez, Pablo Neruda (whom Wright had read at Kenyon), Jorge Guillén, Antonio Machado, and others, prompted Wright's new, freer poems. Amid his awakening to the Spanish-language poets and his re-immersion in the Germans, Wright was completing work on his second book, *Saint Judas* (1959), and beginning to write early versions of the poems that would appear in *The Branch Will Not Break* (1963). In the months after his first visit to the farm, Wright read and translated the German and Spanish-language poets, under the

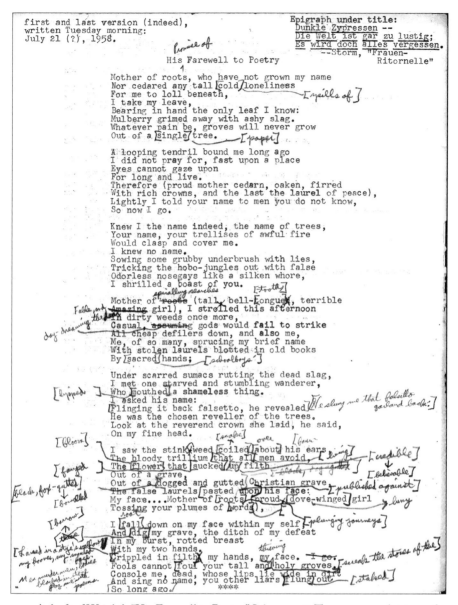

2.4 A draft of Wright's "His Farewell to Poetry," July 21, 1958. The poem, much trimmed, appeared in *The Branch Will Not Break* as "Goodbye to the Poetry of Calcium."

guidance of Bly, and became involved in the production of *The Fifties* with Bly, Carol, and William Duffy as they looked to foreign poets as models for their "new" work. On a larger scale, the collaboration between Wright and Bly brought the poetry of many lesser-known European and South American poets to the consciousness of poets and readers in the United States and started a marvelous rumbling landslide of translation and publication in periodicals and anthologies. Translations of foreign poets who met the criteria for this new poetry filled the pages of *The Fifties*, interspersed with passionate treatises, written mostly by Bly, on the failings of the "ego-ridden verse of English and American modernism." Wright enthusiastically joined Bly in this crusade, feeling that, after the publication of *Saint Judas* (1959), his poetry had come to a "dead end." He had begun to question the validity of the very craft he had worked so hard to perfect. In August of 1958, he wrote to Roethke (the ellipses are Wright's own):

> I have been depressed as hell. My stuff stinks, and you know it. It stinks because it is *competent*. The irony is that, beginning with nothing but absolutely unbearable clumsiness when I was about nineteen years old, I deliberately set out to learn the craft. Well, I seem to have learned it, Good God! . . . I've been cracking my own facility, my competence, my dead and dull iambs, to pieces. What makes this so ironically depressing, as I say, is that I am trapped by the very thing—the traditional technique—which I labored so hard to attain.[51]

In an interview with Michael Andre in 1972, Wright discussed the effect Bly's ideas had on him:

> Robert Bly suggested to me that there is a kind of poetry that can be written. People have written it in some other languages. He said it might be possible to come back to our own language through reading them and translating them, and I think that in one sense this has been the value of translation.[52]

During this second phase of translation of Trakl, Wright mined the poems for the images and their associations that had fascinated him in that Vienna classroom and again in his 1954 Workbook. In the process of translating the poems that would appear in *Twenty Poems of Georg Trakl*, from the summer of 1958 to its publication in 1961, Wright and Bly became focused on the presentation of the image: "to translate the image <u>as</u> <u>image</u>, [Wright's underline] not as a mere equivalent abstraction."

Until meeting Robert Bly, translation was, for the most part, a solitary act for Wright. At Kenyon College, he had occasionally worked on a few translations with Roger Hecht and Robert Mezey, and at the University of Minnesota he had translated several of Rilke's lesser-known poems with Sarah Youngblood, but it was not until he met Bly that he began to think seriously about publishing his translations. Up to then Wright had translated Rilke, Trakl, and the other German poets in order to move inside the poems to discover their secrets. Encountering Bly, who was interested in publishing foreign poets in *The Fifties*, gave Wright an exciting new outlet for the publication of his translations and essays.

From their first meeting, Wright and Bly had in mind the goal of publishing Trakl in book form. Their efforts were not realized for some three years after that meeting, when *Twenty Poems of Georg Trakl* (1961) became the first book under the imprint of Sixties Press, as well as the first volume in English dedicated to the translation of Trakl. Collaborating on the Trakl translations was truly a joint venture. Bly told of how he and Wright would each take different poems, work on them separately, and then come together to help each other revise their versions. Many of the drafts among Wright's papers have comments and notes by both Wright and Bly, showing their attempts to solve the problems of translation. Chapter 7 presents a portfolio and essay representing this lively and important collaboration.

One of the more significant comments on these drafts, part of which was mentioned above, is found on a typed draft of Trakl's "Klage" (Lament) where Wright boldly penned this note below his translation, and transcribed here:

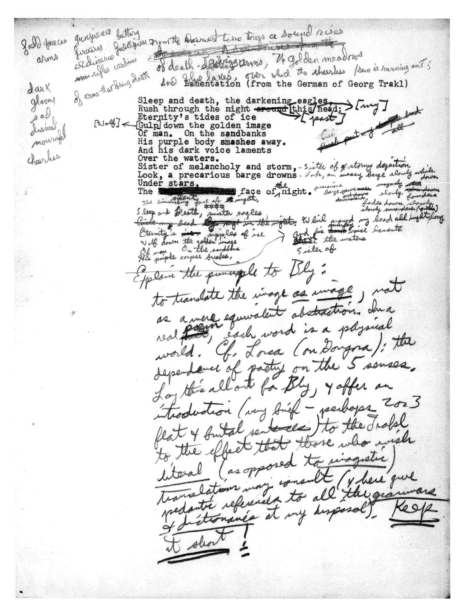

Lamentation (from the German of Georg Trakl)

Sleep and death, the darkening eagles,
Rush through the night around this head:
Eternity's tides of ice
Gulp down the golden image
Of man. On the sandbanks
His purple body smashes away.
And his dark voice laments
Over the waters.
Sister of melancholy and storm,
Look, a precarious barge drowns
Under stars.
The   face of night.

2.5   A typescript of Wright's translation of Trakl's "Lamentation," with notes by Robert Bly and Wright. "Explain the principle to Bly," notes Wright, "to translate the image as image, not as a mere equivalent abstraction."

56

Explain the principle to Bly:

To translate the image <u>as</u> <u>image</u>, not as a mere equivalent abstraction. In a real poem, each word is a physical world. Cf. Lorca (on Góngora): the dependence of poetry on the 5 senses. Lay this all out for Bly, & offer an introduction (very brief—perhaps 2 or 3 flat & brutal sentences) to the Trakl to the effect that those who wish <u>literal</u> (as opposed to <u>imagistic</u>) translations may consult (& here give pedantic references to all the <u>grammars</u> & <u>dictionaries</u> at my disposal). <u>Keep it short</u>! [Wright's underlines][53]

Drafts among Wright's papers show revisions and comments each poet made on the Trakl translations, including those of Carol Bly, whose contribution has been overlooked. Her notes and acute suggestions on a number of drafts demonstrate the important role she played in the translation of the Trakl poems. She also collaborated on the publication of *The Fifties*, while caring for the entire household, later including the four Bly children and frequent visitors, including Wright—with whom she sat many evenings at the kitchen table, listening to him and encouraging him. She also maintained the large garden that produced much of the food for the farm. Even with all of this responsibility, her comments and suggestions appear on many drafts of translations among Wright's papers. Here is a transcription of one extensive handwritten note of hers written at the bottom of a Wright draft of "Grodek," Trakl's last and one of his most powerful poems:

In the first 2 lines, do you think he could be saying
(essentially)
    (sounding)
In the evening the autumn woods are speaking <u>about</u>
deadly weapons—   (blaring)

   —whatever
Die heisse Flamme des Geistes + ?

Today a grimmer agony than that? Feeding the soul's searing fire
—the unborn grandchildren.

Doch stille etc =

I think "the moon's cold" is congealing
the red cloud of smeared blood
     (and that it's in this blood (or cloud) that
the festering God has his home—namely,
  love of murder or death—whatever the terrible
attribute is that the poem's about, in a way)

I said "festering" not as a suggested word but
only because it's a cloud[?] that's going to get
   more rampant than ever at Grodek—like
   gangrene—and it'll show up in our grand
   children even! Something like that.[54]

Carol's comments are substantial and show how closely she was in-
volved in the collaboration between Wright and Bly.

A key to understanding Wright's new poetry was the presence of
silence and solitude he found in Trakl and Rilke. It was the silence he
understood in Trakl that caused Wright in "Echo for the Promise of
Georg Trakl's Life" to call to Trakl: "Hear me, / Father of my sound
. . ." In his introduction to *Twenty Poems of Georg Trakl*, he further
elaborates on his rigorous attentiveness to Trakl's voice:

> I believe that patience is the clue to the understanding of Trakl's
> poems. One does not so much read them as explore them. They
> are not objects which he constructed, but quiet places at the
> edge of a dark forest where one has to sit still for a long time and
> listen very carefully. Then, after all one's patience is exhausted,
> and it seems as though nothing inside the poem will ever make
> sense in the ways to which one has become accustomed by pre-
> vious reading, all sorts of images and sounds come out of the
> trees, or the ponds, or the meadows, or the lone roads—those
> places of awful stillness that seem at the center of nearly every
> poem Trakl ever wrote.[55]

When Wright put a group of translations at the center of his *Collected Poems*, it was as if he were saying as he looked back and gathered his poems: *here is the secret key to my work.* The treasure he found in translation shimmers beneath his own words and connects him to the foreign writers he loved and to the shared music of their languages. In *Selected Poems of Rainer Maria Rilke*, Bly says that the German word "Innigkeit" (inwardness) is so much stronger than the English word and "has the depth of a well where one finds water." That is what Wright found in the poets he translated, from Catullus to Horace, Rilke to Trakl, Char to Apollinaire, and Neruda to Vallejo—a source of deep spiritual sustenance as he drank in their poems.

Wright himself admits to not understanding "the miracles of those images" he was trying to capture, possess, and transform in his own work. In the end, the "tide-suck of that music" is not to be understood, but experienced, and Wright's quest led him to this, the knowledge that his eye, his ear, and his heart must absorb the things of this world, and though he did not often reveal his interest in the German poets, the two poems, "The Quest" and "Sitting in a Small Screenhouse on a Summer Morning," given the power of their position in *Collected Poems*, show us Rilke and Trakl, shimmering beneath his words, spanning like a bridge.

"The Quest" offers a map of the first steps of Wright's journey, written at the culmination of his initial immersion in German poetry in Vienna and revisited later in Roethke's class. The poem resounds with allusions to Rilke's "Orpheus. Eurydike. Hermes."—"twilight chewed the road"—and the *Sonnets to Orpheus*—"careful, quiet ear" and can be read as a rewrite of "Vision and Elegy." Wright even considered including "The Quest" in a manuscript of his first book, *The Green Wall.* The poem was with him from the beginning, although it did not see print until given its place of honor in *Collected Poems.*

"Sitting in a Small Screenhouse on a Summer Morning," the other poem Wright chose to stand at the head of *Collected Poems*, was written nearly ten years after "The Quest." The draft found among Wright's papers was dated June 16, 1962. In it the speaker is alone on the Bly farm, in a "temporary" home, suspended between the screenhouse and the roofless world of the cornfield as he imagines the walk "ten miles" down the road that would take him into South Dakota. This poem, with its irregular lines, has a form freer than "The Quest," more like Wright's poems in *The Branch Will Not Break*, and it brims with Trakl's influence—we hear Trakl and see Trakl-like images—"blue roads"—"a blue horse, dancing / Down a road, alone." The speaker has awakened on a summer morning and takes in everything around him and imagines what is beyond him, where the roads "turn blue"—where he "could have become / A horse, a blue horse, dancing / Down a road alone."

In the poems of Rilke and Trakl and the other German poems he translated early in his career, Wright found something more than prosody, form, and image; he found a strange music, too, which includes silence as part of the sound and sense of poetry. What Trakl once wrote of himself, in a letter to his sister, could also be said of Wright:

> . . . all animated ear that I am, I lie in wait for the melodies which are within me and my winged eye dreams . . . I am my own world, my whole, beautiful world, full of unending melody.[56]

3. Selected German Translations by James Wright

The German translations I found scattered throughout the James Wright Papers (in the Upper Midwest Literary Archive at the University of Minnesota) are central to my work, which chronicles Wright's intense contact with German that began when he was an undergraduate at Kenyon College. This engagement with German poetry continued throughout his career, during which he published individual volumes of translations from Storm, Hesse, and Trakl. From Wright's Kenyon years alone, there are more than one hundred translations from sixteen different German-language poets, in addition to drafts and revised versions of each translation. More than half of the translations from Wright's Kenyon years come from the poetry of Rilke, Heine, and Storm.

This selection represents some of the more than three hundred German translations I gathered in my dissertation *Solitary Apprenticeship: James Wright and German Poetry* (1996). All but three of the selections here have not been collected and published.

Citations and publication history are given at the end of the book in the Sources for Translations.

Saundra Rose Maley

RAINER MARIA RILKE (1875–1926)

from *Erste Gedichte*, 1895

THE WATER HAS DELICATE MELODIES

The water has delicate melodies,
And far away are city and dust;
The treelofts beckon here and there
And I am spent and lost.
The wood is wild, the world is spacious,
My heart is large and luminous,
And my mind lying in the lap of earth
Knows loneliness.

VIGIL

A vigil perilous
   I kept at night
Beside a tenebrous
   Oak locked from sight
Of any wandering one
   Out on the road.
Only the looming moon
   Showered on the tip
Of the oak like God
   Or a woman's lip.

A silver pollen fell
   Against the leaves
And into the pasture well
   Went, as wind breathes,
For the vigil kept
   Was richened over the land;

The moon was a lily that slept
   In God's hand.

Lyrics from *Das Stundenbuch* (*The Book of Hours*), 1905

I, 35

Of little death it is beyond belief,
Whose crown of hair we daily look upon,
He is a sorrow to us and a grief;
That his severity has no relief;
For I still live despite the body gone;
My blood is living as the rose's leaf.

III, 6

O God, give his own death to every one.
The death that from his own life goes,
Wherein he had love, sense, and sadness.

from *Das Buch der Bilder* (*The Book of Images*), 1902–1906

HERBST

Newspapers, written music, the membranes of the world,
fall with skirts and the leaves, fall as from great
    distance, as though withered in heaven's gardens.
They die away and descend, flowing strangely,
    in a reverse bearing like a woman
    having a miscarriage and clinging
    to the life within her as long as she can.

And into the night falls the grievous and heavy earth,
from all the stars into the loneliness.

We all shall fall. This hand here falls.
But look on the others: they all fall into the hand—
    there is ruin in the moving hand

That still is one which this fall, this ruin of autumn landscapes
    includes and protects in its hand as in tender space.

from *Neue Gedichte*, 1907–1908

ORPHEUS, EURYDICE, HERMES

from Wright's unpublished student folio of 1949

It was to the soul as is a mine exotic,
As quiet veins of silver ore they went,
As lode streaks through the darkness. Between roots
Rose the warm blood, going forward to men,
Heavy, as porphyr saw it, to the end of darkness.
Otherwise nothing was red.

An adamant dike was there. Over the void,
Bridges, and that monstrous, gray, blind pond
Which lofty hung over the distant ground
Like a rainy heaven hung over a landscape.
And among meadows, gentle and with a full
Forbearance, appeared the faint streak of a path
Like a long pallor laid down.

Alone along this way they came.

Foremost the slender man in the blue mantle,
Who quietly and impatiently looked ahead.
Without voraciously chewing his own way
In raw, enormous morsels; his hands hung
Heavy and lonely out of the fall of creases
And they no more knew of the facile lyre,
That long had changed back into clumsiness,
Dry tendrils on an oily tree's gray boughs.
His senses were as though utterly sundered,
His vision ran before him like a hound,
And turned and then returned from far away,
And stood in wait for the next order of turning,—
His musical ear remained behind, like scent.
Sometimes it seemed to him as though it reached
Up to both of the others in their going,
Who should have followed this whole declivity.

Then again it was only his rising echo
And the wind around his mantle there behind him.
But to himself he said: they should have come;
Loudly he spoke, and heard his dying voice.
They should have come here, they were only two,
Who went so anxiously. Could he have turned
But once himself (were such a looking back
Not all the dissolution of creation,
That was at first accomplished), he might have seen
Faintly the pair pursuing him in silence:

To the god of going and of far messages,
The cap of the traveler over his bright eyes,
Bearing a slim rod ahead of the beloved
With flapping wings on the rudders of his feet;
And with his left hand given: to her.
She who was so beloved, that from a lyre
Issued more moans than from a mourning woman,

And a whole world came out of its long wailing,
In which all things existed: valley and forest,
Village and path, field and river and beast;
And she was for that wailing world entirely
As for the other earth a sun may be,
Along with which a starry heaven goes,
A mournful heaven with disfigured stars—:
She who was so beloved.

But well she went along at that god's hand,
On a way enclosed by long funereal bands,
Unsure though gently and not impatiently.
For she was like a high hope in herself
And thought not of the man who led the way,
Nor of the path behind her to the living.
She stayed within herself. And being dead
She realized to be a plenitude.
Like a fruit plucked of sweetness and of darkness,

So was she full of her tremendous death,
Therefore complete, and so she gathered nothing.

And she was bearing a new maidenhood,
And was untouched in silence; for her sex
Was too like a young bloom against the evening,
And so much were her hands to marriage
Unused, that from the light-foot god himself
The endless, delicate, summons-answering touch
Pained her extremely by its intimacy.

Already she was no longer a blond wife,
Building chords often in the poet's songs,
No more of the wide bed's urgency and fragrance,
And of that man the property no more,
Already she had loosened like long hair
And had surrendered like a fallen rain,
Divided like a hundred-paneled store.

Already she was root.
And when suddenly, rashly
The god stayed her with sorrow in his outcry
And spoke the words: He had turned himself around—,
She did not understand, and easily said: Who?

But distant, dark beyond the lucid passage,
Stood a someone whose dimmed countenance
Could not be recognized. He stood and gazed,
While on the ribbon of the pastoral path
With trustful eyes the god of messages
Quietly turned about to follow the form
Already going back by the same road,
On the way enclosed by long funereal bands,
Unsure though gently and not impatiently.

from *Die Gedichte*, 1922–1926

PALM OF THE HAND

Palm of the hand. Sole that walks no more
Except through feeling. It opens itself upwards
And in its mirror
Gathers the roads of heaven, themselves
Become wanderers.
It has learned to walk on water
When it becomes
Transformer of all pathways
Walking over the well-springs.
It steps into other hands,
It makes its own kind
Into landscape:
Wanders and arrives in them,
Fills them with arrivals.

from *Die Frühen Gedichte*, 1909

WENN DIE UHREN SO NAH . . .

When the clocks nearby
Strike as if their own hearts were beating
And the things with timid
Voices ask one another:
Are you there?—:

Then I am not the same man who awoke this morning;
the night gives me a new name,
which no one to whom I spoke by daylight
learns of, without deep dread—

Every door
In me opens
Inward . . .

And then I know that nothing passes away,
no gesture and no prayer

(things are too heavy for that);
my whole childhood stands
always around me.
I am never alone.
Many who lived before me
and struggled forth from me,
wove,
wove
at my being.

And if I sit near you
and tell you softly: *I suffered*—

Who knows who
Murmurs with me?

HEINRICH HEINE (1797–1856)

Kleider Machen Lause: ein Liederkranz

"CLOTHES MAKE THE MAN: A SONG CYCLE":
SOME IMITATIONS OF HEINRICH HEINE'S GERMAN

I. Dear John
The letter that you wrote me
To say that you were done
Had twelve close-written pages,
With both sides scribbled on.

It had twelve pages, dearie;
The envelope was large.
Employers are not so windy
In giving a discharge.

II. Despair
I thought I could not bear it;
My heart is healing now,
And, as you see, I bore it,
But do not ask me how.

Alack! I should have heeded
My anguished toes themselves.
I cannot wear elevens:
My feet are built for twelves.

III. De Profundis

They gave me all kinds of good advice;
They said I should raise my downcast eyes,
And promised me that, if I would wait,
They would protect me against my fate.

But all their fine protection brought
Were hopeful eyes and an empty gut.
Then a marvelous fellow came and said
He would make sure that I was fed.

Marvelous fellow! Thank God I met him.
The hell with the others, I'll never forget him.
I long to embrace him, but never can;
For I myself am this excellent man.

IV. Intrigue

Past ruin'd Ilion Helen lies,
Heroic wars are finished;
The gods have, in a various guise,
Appreciably diminished.

There is no Hero, by the way,
To watch Leander drown.
We literate lovers of today
Snivel, and write it down.

This writing takes the edges off
The old barbaric passion:
We wish we bellowed loud of love
In ancient singers' fashion.

Dearly beloved little heart,
Helen let Paris rape her.

We cannot take the true love's part
Unless we banish paper.

from *Buch der Lieder*, 1827

SEA GHOST (SEEGESPENST)
But I lay at the edge of the ship,
And gazed with dreaming eyes
Down into the water clear as a mirror,
And stared deeper and deeper—
Till deep, on the floor of the sea,
Beginning like a dusky mist,
Yet gradually secure in their color,
Churches with vaulted arches and steeples appeared
And finally, sunclear, a whole city,
Ancient and Netherlandish,
And bustling with men.
Prudent men, cloaked in black,
With white throatruffles and honorable chains
And long swords and long faces,
Strode over the swarming marketplace,
To the highstaired town hall,
Where the stony image of the emperor
Kept watch with sceptre and sword.
Nearby, before the long tiers of the houses,
Where the mirror-gleaming windows are
And the lindens trimmed like pyramids,
The silkenrustling virgins move,
Slim little bodies, flowerfaces
Chastely enclosed in black little caps
And the gold hair spilling forth.

Variegated companions in Spanish dress
Strut past and nod.
Yearstricken women,
In brown fading raiment,
Songbooks and garlands of roses in their hands,

Hasten with tripping steps,
To the great cathedral,
Urged by the pealing of bells
And the roaring tone of the organ.

To me myself reaches the mysterious
Paroxysm of distant sound!
Endless yearning, deep melancholy
Stealthily creeps upon my heart,
My heart scarcely healed;—
It seems to me as though its wounds
Were kissed by the beloved lips,
And were shedding blood again,
Hot red droplets
That fall down long and slowly
Upon an old house there underneath
In the deep city of the sea,
Upon the old highgabled house,
Melancholy and deserted,
Now that under the window
A maiden sits,
Her head thrust into her arms,
Like a poor neglected child—

And I know you, poor neglected child!
So deep, seadeep
You hid yourself from me
Out of a childish whim,
And could not return,
And sat alien among alien people
For centuries,
While I, with my soul full of grief,
Sought you across the whole earth,
And sought you always,
You always beloved
Lost for so long,
Finally found—

I have found you and gaze again
Into your sweet face,
Your bright and loyal eyes,
The dear smile—
And never will I lose you again,
And I shall come down to you,
And with outspread arms
Crush you to my heart—

But just at the right moment
The captain grasps me by the foot,
And draws me back from the railing of the ship,
And cries, irritably laughing:

Take it easy, buddy.

THEODOR STORM (1817–1888)

WOMAN'S RITORNELLE

Blossoming myrtle tree—
I was hoping to gather your sweet fruit;
The blossoms fell; now I can see I was wrong.

Quick, shrivelling winds—
I went out looking for the footprints I left as a child
Along your windbreak, but I could not find them.

Nutmeg herb,
You blossomed once in my great-grandmother's garden;
That was a place a long way from the world, over there.

Dark cypresses—
The world is too interested in gaiety;
It will all be forgotten.

ORPHAN

I am a rose, pluck me again.
Naked my roots to the wind and rain.

No! Go away and leave me loose.
I am no flower, I am no rose.

My coat is blown as the wind is wild;
I am a fatherless motherless child.

WALTHER VON DER VOGELWEIDE (CA. 1170–1230)

OWÊ WAR SINT VERSWUNDEN ALLIU MÎNIU JÂR?

Alas, where have all my years gone to?
Has my life been just a dream, or is it real?
All those things that I used to think stood for something,
Did they really stand for anything?
It seems as though I have been asleep without knowing it.
Now I have wakened, and all looks strange to me,
That I used to know as well as my own hand . . .

JOHANN WOLFGANG VON GOETHE (1749–1832)

NATURE AND ART

Nature and art appear to be;
Before one knows, they meet to clasp and fold,
And also I their unity behold,
And both arise before me equally.

If first we toil at time through measured hours,
With labor and spirit bind ourselves to art,
Nature may freely glow within the heart.
An integrated troubling should be ours.

With any education is it so:
Spirits ungoverned surely will have failed
Attainment of the purest height to be.

Who would be lofty, learn to labor low.
In boundaries the master is revealed,
And only law itself can make us free.

Nü Bin Ich Erwachet (Walter von der Vogelweide,
O wê war sint verswunden
alliu mîniu jâr?)

~~Wet Met, d help~~

[still]

Under the broken tree
The man sat down with me.
~~Still?~~ I can see him there:
The long winter of air
~~Piles the drifts of his hair.~~ → *lazily drifts his hair.*
I am young, he is old,
And the light shrinks over the field.
~~Beyond the cornshucks he lives~~
~~In a house where a woman lives,~~
A daughter too old for me
To marry, ~~though she be lonely;~~ *is ugly; and she is ugly;*
~~too,~~ grown to a snow-mossed rock,
I watch the age of the dark,
And another winter, fall
Over the old man, over all:
Field, stubble, house,
And the woman's ~~hidden~~ face.   *delete*
I know she sleeps up there,
~~I know she sleeps for despair~~
[dm]   ~~Of~~ a winter she cannot bear.
She knows I am sitting awake
With an old man on a rock
To watch the daylight break.

* * *

The daylight broke, that day,
~~Or bent,~~ while she grew gray
And died, for all I know,
Years, years ago.
[She never learned to...] →   ~~The gray drift buried her, had~~
~~The woman who could not bear~~
~~The cold or the sudden fire.~~
~~And neither can I, this year,~~
adrift, graying, down?   ~~This year, when time is gone~~
And I sit on another stone,
~~Older myself, and alone --~~
Except for one old man,
Here since my life began,
[who passed]   Who hid from me in the shade;   3/c
[and saw the moves I made,] →   ~~Watched all the steps I made,~~
And saw me falter, ~~and crept~~   3/c
[From where he slept,] →   ~~Out of the dark, where he slept,~~   [pit]
And sat with me on a stone,
And sat in me on a stone,
~~Winter and spring both done.~~
space   ~~And my youth is gone.~~
Winter is nearly gone.

* * * *

3.1   A draft of an imitation of the minnesinger Walther von der Vogelweide's "Owê war sint verswunden alliu mîniu jâr?," which Wright published in 1959 in *Audience* as "A Man in the North: Nü Bin Ich Erwachet."

EDUARD MÖRIKE (1804–1875)

SOUL, REMEMBER

A fir tree greens, and where
Who knows? in woodlands.
A rose bush buds, who says,
And in what garden?
They are already chosen,
Soul, remember,
Upon thy grave to nourish
And to burgeon.

Two small black horses graze
Among the meadows;
They trip back home to town
With merry gambols.
Straightway they will go prancing
With thy body,
Maybe, maybe before
Upon their hooves
The iron darkens and dies
That I see sparkling.

IM FRÜHLING

Here upon the hill of spring I lie:
The white cloud becomes my wing,
And the one bird before me flies.
O only beloved one, tell me
Where you are that with you I may be.
Yet you of the air, you have no house.

Wide as sunlight flowers my mind is poised,
Desiring,
Desiring and leaping
Upward in love and hope.
O Spring, what have you wished?
And when will I be hushed?

Hush now, I see the cloud meandering,
The wandering river.
And golden deep, the sun's kiss presses
Its warmth in my veins, my balanced ears.
My eyes, drunken with wonder,
Close beneath such kisses.
In the long tone of bees my ears go under.

I trouble this and trouble that,
I long for and I know not rightly what:
Half of desire and half a wailing rime.
O heart, heart, tell what you weave
From an old dusk in the green limbs remembering?
—A day without its name, fled into time . . .

HERMANN HESSE (1877–1962)

LONELY EVENING

In the empty bottle and in the glass
Flickers the lustre of the candle;
It is cold in the room.
Delicate in the grass outdoors, the rain.
Now again you lie for a brief rest
Chilly and solemn again.
Morning returns, and evening
Always comes again
But never you.

BROTHER DEATH

As you came to me once,
You do not forget me,
And the anguish is ended,
Of the fetters free.

Still you seem strange and distant,
Death dear brother,

You stand like a cool star
Above my sorrow.

But you will be nearer
As your flame overpours—
Come, beloved, I am here,
Take me, I am yours.

Strange, in the fog to wander.
Lonely is every bush and stone,
Scarcely a tree can see another,
Every one is alone.

The world was full of friends for me,
When my life had light;
Now where the fog is falling,
None is in sight.

Surely no man is wise
Who will not understand
The dark that inescapably
Parts him from the land.

Strange, in the fog to wander:
To life when none
Of all men knows another.
Everyone is alone.

GEORG TRAKL (1887–1914)

Three unpublished Trakl translations

TRANSFIGURATION

When evening comes,
Trust softly in a blue face.
A small bird sings in the tamarind tree.

A gentle monk
Folds his numb hands together.
A white angel haunts images of Mary.

Dark as the night, a garland
Of violets, grain, and purple clusters of grapes
Is the pattern of the year.

Before your feet
The graves of the dead come open,
When you rest your forehead in your silver hands.

Silently the autumnal
Moon lodges upon your mouth,
Drunk with the opium of dark music;
Blue flower,
That chimes softly in yellowed stone.

THE WANDERER

Always the white night leans on the hill;
Where the poplar ascends into silver sounds,
There are stars and stones.
Sleeping, the footbridge arches above the mountain rapids
A dead face follows the boy,
Sickle-moon in the rose-colored gorge,

Distant shepherds singing their praises. In ancient rock
The toad stares out of crystal eyes,
The wind wakens into blossom, the bird-voice of one who seems
    dead,
And footsteps gently grow green in the woods.

This recalls tree and animal. Slow stairs of moss,
And the moon,
That sinks shining into waters of grief.

It returns and wanders along the green shore,
Weaving on a black gondola through the fallen city.

3.2   A handwritten draft of Wright's translation of Trakl's "The Wanderer" from July 11, 1959. The translation never appeared in print.

THE RETURN HOME

The coolness of a dark year,
Grief and hope
Held off by cyclopean stone,
A mountain emptied of men,
The golden wilderness of autumn,
Evening cloud—
Purity!

Crystal childhood gazes
Out of blue eyes;
Under dark spruce trees
Love, hope,
Where dew drops from red eyelids
Into the stiff grass—
No one can stop it.

There! the gold footbridge
Crumbling apart in the snow
Of the precipice!
By night the valley breathes
Blue coolness,
Belief, hope!
Good evening, bare graveyard!

AMEN

Decayed bodies gliding through the rotten room;
Shadows on yellow wallpaper; in dark mirrors arches
The ivory solemnity of our hands.

Brown pearls run through the dead fingers.
In the silence
The blue-poppy eyes of an angel are opening.

The evening is also blue;
The hour of our dying off, shadows of Israel,
That dims into a small brown garden.

JOSEPH VON EICHENDORFF (1788–1857)

JOY OF DEATH

Before he sank into the blue flood,
The swan still dreams and sings; drunken
On death, weary of summer, the earth
In the cessation of its blooming
Lets all its fire glow in the clusters of grapes;

Aug. 9, 59.

to   Otero, We'll in the
fled the hammer's [stroke] of [crystal], the breast
[awaits] [effects] that grief

                    [Placide Au]

Aug. 11, 59:   These translations of Trakl are done:

1. Transfigurations
2. "Bobbing thru fallen city... etc."
3. The Song of the Dead's Crumbling
4. Birth
5. Trumpets
6. Lament
7. Amp
8. In the Swamp
9. My Heart Towards Evening
10. Landscape
11. De Profundis
12. Amen
13. Summer (R. Bly)
14. The Sun (R. Bly)
15. Sleep
16. The Return Home
17. The Evening

3.3   A page from Wright's notebook, dated August 11, 1959, with a notation:
"These translations of Trakl are done."

The sun, scattering sparks in its setting,
Still gives the earth a glow to drink,
Until, star by star, all the intoxicated ones,
The wonderful night disappears.

LONELINESS

Praying for warmth amid an isle of cold
Forests of frosted firs desolate,
Your frail arms fail to embrace the lonely old
Wind, so you turn among the roses late
In autumn whose aged fire might keep you warm;
But there you find each individual rose
Pursuing death inside its private storm;
And down bare village houses the wind blows.

Strange faces watch you from gray cottages;
Bone fingers echo, from inside, the breeze
Booming and hammering at each blunt, bald head;
Wind stops—then stealthily sneaks up the street
To stir brown dust while your white lips repeat.

4. A Fine Weave of Voices: Translation, Whitman, and James Wright's New Style

JEFFREY KATZ

Even while James Wright was preparing his second book *Saint Judas* (1959) for Wesleyan University Press, he was trying out the new poems that would characterize his next collection, eventually published by Wesleyan as *The Branch Will Not Break* (1963). In fact, twenty-eight of the poems that were finally published in *The Branch* were written between 1959 and early 1961. This was a time of great personal turbulence for the poet—his continuing struggle with alcohol, the divorce from his first wife, Liberty, and a breakdown requiring hospitalization— and a whirlwind of deep work in translation. From the summer of 1958 through the early 1960s he made hundreds of versions of poems by Vallejo, Neruda, Lorca, Trakl, Jiménez, and Guillén, and wrote dozens of excited letters about the translations and his own new work. As the letters make clear, the translations were creating an urgency in him, a crystalizing pressure of new life and new form.

In his valuable study *James Wright: The Poetry of a Grown Man*, Kevin Stein characterizes the postwar literary history of the 1940s and 1950s—with the T. S. Eliot–influenced New Critics in one camp and those influenced by William Carlos Williams in the other—as the "poetics of polarization." He describes the poles as a poetics of "containment" and a poetics of "vulnerability." And he shows clearly, by examining *Amenities of Stone*, the unpublished precursor manuscript to *The Branch Will Not Break*, that Wright had tents pitched in both camps, shedding considerable light on the process of Wright's agonistic movement from the poems of his first two books toward those of his third. The process shows Wright's careful assembling of the work for publication, mixing and remixing more than a hundred poems—including translations from Rilke and Goethe—before he achieved the right balance. It is the important story of Wright moving away from the orderly forms and meter that acted as a protective distancing from experience, and toward more direct engagement with the world, more vulnerability, more empathy, and more openness.[1]

The so-called surrealism of his new work delighted some of Wright's readers at the time, and enraged others. Neither camp, though, sufficiently saw the continuity in his poems from *The Green Wall* onward, which was borne by the poet's restless, exploratory poetics, pushing out the limits of his art and the limits of his truth-telling. Wright may have mostly turned away from rhyme and traditional meter after his first two books, but, as he often insisted, there is always form, various and delicate.

Just at the point of this turning away Wright met Robert and Carol Bly. By them he felt encouraged in his enthusiasms for Trakl and the ever-returning voice of Walt Whitman, and he dove headlong into the Spanish and Latin American poets. Together Wright and Bly were looking for new ways of working with poems and approaching consciousness, ways of letting themselves down into a dark beneath logic and orderly literary conventions. They sought out encounters with a language and culture that were strange to them. They made working in this strange territory into a way to reshape their own poems.

As Wright and Bly were beginning their work on translating Trakl, they were also carrying on a vigorous correspondence about the "new style" announced by Bly in the first issue of *The Fifties*. In these exchanges Wright asks for clarification of what the editors mean by the "old style," and provides his own sturdy dissent from Bly's broad dismissal of iambics, while trying to tease out what is really at the spoiling core of American postwar poetry. In a letter to Bly from July 23, 1958 (*AWP* 121) he writes:

Is the use of iambic rhythm as such necessarily a sign that American poetry is "moving backward"? . . . Now, look, are [Karl] Shapiro's poems [for example] written in the old style because he uses iambs, or because of his imagery? . . . you say the deepest threat to the "new imagination" is what you call "dying language—that is, totally without images." Now, I am certain that I know what you mean by imagery, and I am completely convinced that your definition of dying language is clear and true.[2]

For Wright the failure of the "old style" is a failure of courage that is tied in his mind to the poet's willingness to look into his own depths, to trust the poetry with his deepest feelings, and to trust the images with exposing these feelings. The letter continues:

His language is dying, in your sense—for imagery is not simply the prosaic photographing of the surfaces of things, but the verbal complexity created by the passionately committed imagination—a complexity which thus contains both the "imagination and terror" and also the poet's creative revelation of what this terror means. Please note that I don't say the poet's statement or gloss on the terror, but his revelation of its meaning . . .[3]

Below is an unpublished draft from 1962 of a poem titled "A Small Elegy at Night in the Country." It is one of a group of soundings out of lines about an afternoon in a chicken house on the Bly farm finally realized as the lovely poem "Sitting in a Small Screenhouse on a Summer Morning," published later that year in the New Yorker. Many years later it was placed by the poet with "The Quest" at the head of his Collected Poems. The urgent notation that follows the fourteen-line poem is a lucid reflection on just the issues he and Bly had been struggling with since 1958—the struggle away from rhetoric and ornament toward a "true imagination," described as a vigorous contest requiring the utmost courage. Here is a transcription of Wright's notation:

Note (later in afternoon, March 6):

This poem contains a clear (though, as usual for me, & as Robt. has been watching patiently for, about 3 years) problem of cutting.

Now, shall I entirely delete the 4 lines which I've penciled in brackets above? I think so. But I'm not sure. [If the answer is yes, then I am learning. If no, then I have to submerge again. But I shd record the fact that I am happy to see & feel the problem!]

1. If I leave them stand, they provide a contrast (footprints) with the "smooth snow," etc. of line 11.

2. But they also distract the imagination from the scene, the setting of the poem in the present moment—and that moment is everything—isn't it? (Damn, that question! If I could truly answer it—if I had courage enough—I could become a poet. I would like very much to be a poet. I really would.)

To keep the issue clear: I would reduce the typescript above to a single line, if such would let the poem emerge. But that's just it, that's as far as I've been able to struggle so far. I am not afraid to abandon rhetoric, but I still can't judge which is rhetoric & which is true imagination! (i.e. I'm still afraid to judge!)

OK. I'll send this page as it is to Robt. & Carol. But I can't [undecipherable] letting even the most beloved friends decide for me!

For Wright, this early exchange is also about what in a poem creates its music—some combination of personal rhythm and imagery—a combination that he had found in his reading of Trakl. He closes his letter with a brilliant example from Hart Crane, which keeps the door on iambics open just a crack:

Every rhythm must be new and original, if it is to contain genuine imagery. Right? Or am I missing the point? But if this is

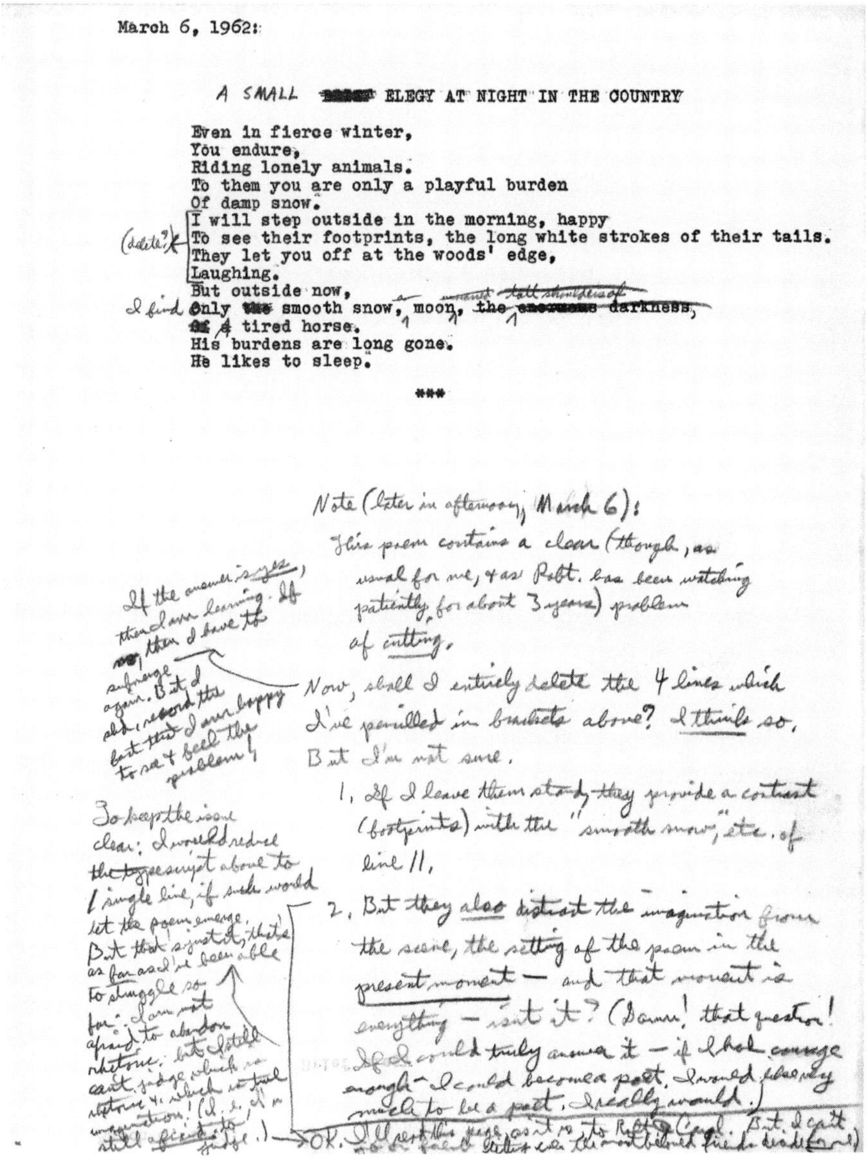

March 6, 1962:

A SMALL ~~ELEGY~~ ELEGY AT NIGHT IN THE COUNTRY

Even in fierce winter,
You endure,
Riding lonely animals.
To them you are only a playful burden
Of damp snow.
I will step outside in the morning, happy
(delete?) To see their footprints, the long white strokes of their tails.
They let you off at the woods' edge,
Laughing.
But outside now,
I find Only ~~the~~ smooth snow, moon, ~~the enormous~~ darkness,
~~of a~~ tired horse.
His burdens are long gone.
He likes to sleep.

***

[Handwritten note, right side:]

Note (later in afternoon, March 6):

This poem contains a clear (though, as usual for me, & as Robt. has been watching patiently for about 3 years) problem of cutting.

Now, shall I entirely delete the 4 lines which I've pencilled in brackets above? I think so, But I'm not sure.

1. If I leave them standing they provide a contrast (footprints) with the "smooth snow", etc. of line 11,

2. But they also distract the imagination from the scene, the setting of the poem in the present moment — and that moment is everything — isn't it? (Damn! that question! If I could truly answer it — if I had courage enough — I could become a poet. I would so very much to be a poet, I really would.)

[Handwritten note, left side:]

If the answer is yes, then I am learning. If no, then I have to splurge again. But I do not regard the problem but that I am happy to see & feel the problem!

To keep the issue clear: I would reduce the typescript above to 1 single line, if such would let the poem emerge. But that's just it, that's as far as I've been able to struggle so far. I am not afraid to abandon rhetoric, but I still can't judge which is rhetoric & which is real imagination! (i.e. I'm still afraid to judge.)

OK. I'll rest this page as it is, to Robt. (God. But I can't...)

4.1 A typescript from March 6, 1962, with Wright's notes describing his "problem of cutting" and his struggle away from rhetoric and ornament toward a "true imagination."

the point about rhythm, then I want to ask if you do or do not think it is possible to build a new and original rhythm on the basis of the iambic measure . . .[4]

Here is Crane in a passage which I have always thought magnificent in its imagery:

The phonographs of hades in the brain
Are tunnels that re-wind themselves, and love
A burnt match skating in a urinal . . .

But the passage is iambic—isn't it? Somehow the great image helps to build a new rhythm on the iambic measure? . . .[5]

Bly responds in a letter dated August 1, 1958, by elaborating on his *Fifties* editorial, making the point that iambics succeeded beautifully in the old life but were inappropriate for the new life of postwar America because they constrained perception of it and the psychic life of individuals:

The old form is perfectly good in itself, for its own life—but when it slyly continues to exist in a time of totally new life, it serves only to dim our perception of that new life . . . Every meter, iambic among them, carries with it subconsciously an entire group of attitudes, emotions, perceptions, even subject matter. If then a poet adopts the iambic, he is directed by that itself to certain attitudes and subjects, and his range becomes narrower; as that happens, he sees less and less of the actual life that surrounds him . . . I went through that myself, and breaking myself of it was like rising from the dead . . . as the perception lessens under pressure of the iamb and its 17th century mind, perception of oneself also lessens; we know less and less who we are; but any personal rhythm comes directly out of ourself, like a river from dark rocks . . .[6]

The exchange of letters that summer is the bright background of their friendship and search for a new style consistent with new life. Their work both on translations and their own new work, begun just a few weeks later, pulled James Wright free of the collapsed building of his early work and his exile in Minneapolis.

His work with translations would give Wright greater access to his own tenderness, anger, melancholy, and reverence by way of just such a personal rhythm, without the constraint of what he called "rhetoric." In other words, he found in the Spanish and Latin American poets in particular a tonal directness, a language highly sophisticated, but left "unmanaged" by the intellect and its New Critical partners—irony, tension, and paradox. He sought language more open to reality in all its variousness. Writing about his early work on a Lorca poem, "Malagueña," in an unpublished letter dated February 1959, the poet says:

> Oh, if only I could learn it. They have dropped all the rhetoric and gone straight to the truth of the soul itself and insisted that the heart is true, that we have no right to reason it away, and they can drop the rhetoric (which I have so often used as a mere defense against experience) because they are not afraid.
> But I'm not afraid either! I just realized it again—I'm not afraid.[7]

The story of the making of *The Branch Will Not Break* would not be complete, though, without noting how deliberately this exacting craftsman established a rich bass line of German voices signaling his earliest efforts to find his own poetic voice. As published, *The Branch* had several notable German markers: first, the book's epigraph from Heine's "Aus alten Märchen winkt es"; second, the inclusion of Wright's translation of lines from Goethe's "Harzreise im Winter" published as "Three Stanzas from Goethe"; third, the epigraph from Theodor Storm for Wright's important poem "Goodbye to the Poetry of Calcium"; and fourth, the deep echo of Rilke in the final line of "Lying in a Hammock at William Duffy's Farm in Pine Island, Minnesota."

By deploying these markers it's as if Wright is saying: This book is new, but behind the new kind of poems here is what I've been trying to say all along about loss and loneliness and the redemptive promise of love. The Heine epigraph and the lines from Goethe—both of which had been transformed into love songs by Schumann and Brahms—are prayers for love: to gladden and quicken the speaker's heart. Wright took his epigraph to "Goodbye to the Poetry of Calcium" from the last stanza of his translation of Storm's "Frauen Ritornelle," a poem of a vanished world, of unattainable beauty. The poem's speaker, like those in the lines from Heine and Goethe and in so many of Wright's own poems, is too late; "the self-seeker [who] finds nothing." Again and again the speaker in Wright's poems intuits that the world is "immeasurably alive and good," but cannot sustain the feeling. He always feels the line of "dark cypresses" along the edge of the yard that he cannot overcome. The last of these markers is the echo of Rilke's famous line from "The Archaic Torso of Apollo": "You must change your life" / "Du musst dein Leben ändern," which becomes a famous line in Wright's poem "Lying in a Hammock": "I have wasted my life." Where Rilke's line is provocative, cautionary, Wright's is confessional, and like Heine's and Goethe's speakers, despairing that the vision he has been vouchsafed may be an illusion.

Around the same time that he was working on the translations of Trakl, Lorca, Vallejo, Neruda, and Jiménez, and the poems that would go into *The Branch Will Not Break*, he was also writing an important and beautiful essay, "The Delicacy of Walt Whitman," which he presented at The English Institute conference in September of 1961 at Columbia University. In it he reminds us that Whitman was in many ways working with the same relation of old forms to new forms in 1855 as Wright was a hundred years later. The question of form is crucially bound up for both poets with their relationship to the past and to the future. "Whitman," says Wright,

> realizes that the past has existed. He also understands how the past continues to exist: it exists in the present, and comes into living form only when some individual man is willing to challenge it . . . He knows that the past exists, and he knows that, as a poet and as a man, he has a right to live. His duty to the past is precisely this: to have the courage to live and to create his own poetry . . . This is the great way of learning from the noble spirits of the past. And the most difficultly courageous way of

asserting the shape and meaning of one's own poetry and one's own life is to challenge and surpass those very traditions and masters whom one can honestly respect.[8]

Wright continues, drawing from the Preface to the 1855 Edition of *Leaves of Grass*, to describe what form means to Whitman (and to himself):

> The rhythm and uniformity of perfect poems shows the free growth of metrical laws, and buds from them as unerringly and loosely as lilacs and roses on a bush, and takes shapes as compact as the shapes of chestnuts and oranges.[9]

Wright then adds his own elaboration to this well-known passage by reading Whitman's "I heard you solemn-sweet pipes" and then by working out how precise Whitman is being with his comparison of "shapes of oranges and chestnuts" to poetic form and metrical laws:

> Whitman first tries to make sure that we will not confuse his poetic forms with the rules of grammar; and then he lets his images grow, one out of another . . .
>
> It is this kind of formal growth that, I believe, gives special appropriateness to Whitman's mention of "shapes as compact as the shapes of chestnuts and oranges." These fruits do indeed have shapes—delicate shapes indeed. And they are compact, not diffuse. Their life depends on their form, which grows out of the forms of blossoms, which, in turn grew out of the forms of seeds.[10]

He might have followed the metaphor a little further and said, too, that this formal growth will show forth sometimes as shapely as a chestnut, sometimes as loose as a lilac bush, according to their natures. The point is to observe, to see how they will grow, not to make them part of a system, but to be patient until their brilliance comes forth.

Wright never left Whitman, despite his academic colleagues' neglect of Whitman's voice throughout the 1950s. For years, he says, "I have loved Whitman in secret. If I mentioned him, and his art, I was sneered at. So I bided my time. And now, just at the moment when I was absolutely alone and could not hide from my own soul's duty any more, I discovered what has happened to the tradition of Whitman. It is alive to the south of us."

A few pages later in the essay, Wright becomes more specific about what he means by the "south of us." He names Lorca's "Ode to Walt Whitman," and adds that the spirit of Whitman is everywhere present among the Spanish and South American poets. Wright goes on to identify the form that they have discovered, following Whitman, that seeks an expression not based on argument but on the imagination's development, a music not based exclusively on meter but on the correspondences of images, a deeper kind of rhyming. He describes it almost breathlessly as "the enormously courageous willingness to leap from one image into the unknown, in sheer faith that the next image will appear in the imagination."[11] He might, in fact, be describing Whitman's practice from any one of his familiar "catalogs" like this one, for instance, from Section 15 of "Song of Myself," in *Leaves of Grass*:

> The pure contralto sings in the organloft,
> The carpenter dresses his plank. . . . the tongue of his foreplane
>   whistles its wild ascending lisp,
> The married and unmarried children ride home to their thanks-
>   giving dinner,
> The pilot seizes the king-pin, he heaves down with a strong arm,
> The mate stands braced in the whaleboat, lance and harpoon are
>   ready,
> The duck-shooter walks by silent and cautious stretches,

This willingness to make the leap from one image into the unknown is, Wright says, underwritten by craft: "Because without craft, by which I mean the active employment of the intelligence, the imagination, that mysterious and frightening thing, cannot come free."[12]

But notice the various facets of Whitman's catalog practice at work. What are the implications of this "willingness to leap from one image into the unknown?" One is that the catalog of images one after another demonstrates abundance and particularity. What is beautiful about it is its variety. This is the world thick with detail, but no detail is subordinate to the rest. So this message on the subject of poetic technique is at the same time a message about social order and its replacement by the mutuality and interdependence of persons, and this Wright sees as Whitman's essential and radical empathy: "I am the man . . . I suffered . . . I was there." Whitman is here working on a fundamental question that is at the core of Wright's poems, too: What is the relationship of feeling—both apperception by way of the senses and feeling as empathy—to human existence?

A second and related implication would be the answer to this question: What are the features of consciousness that construct a field or grid of perception and representation that gives priority to seeing/ observing before knowing, making, and writing? This consciousness gives priority to plurality and diversity and variety (again ideally representing the wished-for social order). The contours of the catalog throughout "Song of Myself" show this: the world is too big, too fast, too various to ever be completely known.

Perhaps an even larger question is: *who* is represented? Emerson's lecture series, "Representative Men," was one of the many popular lectures in the nineteenth century designed to instruct citizens by way of exemplary men (of course, men), give a view of steady progress, demonstrate the need for heroic leadership, and celebrate the aura of a golden past. Whitman's view of inclusion, of what is worthy of representation—and, clearly, Wright's view as well—might be best summed up in two places in section 15 of "Song of Myself":

The prostitute draggles her shawl, her bonnet bobs on her tipsy
    and pimpled neck,
The crowd laugh at her blackguard oaths, the men jeer and wink
    to each other,
(Miserable! I do not laugh at your oaths nor jeer you,)

and the section's final lines looking back not only over this section, but out over the whole poem:

> And these one and all tend inward to me, and I tend outward
>   to them,
> And such as it is to be of these more or less I am.

For Wright, representation meant visibility, inclusion, reverence ever since the first poems in *The Green Wall*. He says over and over with Whitman: "I am less the reminder of property or qualities, and more the reminder of life." Look particularly at the many poems about persons too easily excluded from society like "To a Fugitive," "Sappho," "A Gesture by a Lady with an Assumed Name," "A Poem about George Doty in the Death House," "Morning Hymn to a Dark Girl," and others from this collection. There are dozens of others appearing in every one of his books until his last, *Two Citizens*.[13]

Wright writes under the aegis of love—however ungovernable, however imperfect, however endlessly impenetrable. And the aim of Eros, he would say, after Freud in *An Outline of Psychoanalysis*, is "to establish ever greater unities and to preserve them thus—in short, to bind together . . ." His dreams in these poems are dreams of rescue, dreams of recovery, ways through dark corridors of wind and leaf and wave to some kind of freedom. This is not a painless, protected precinct, but a freedom where one sees all things human at a human scale—frailty, courage, joy, longing, praise, shame, fear—and the cost is enormous. Yet it is bravely undertaken in his poems—this binding together—for the sake of love. For Wright, the central drama, the ethos driving his work, is the inseparability of love and language.

Whitman is looking over his shoulder while Wright works out the issues of form, the growth of images, and appropriate equivalents of imagination in Vallejo, in Neruda, and in Trakl as well. Again and again he goes to these poets for what they can show him about the further development of his art, the human scale, and tenderness.

Wright could have been thinking of these lines from his translation of Vallejo's "The Distant Footsteps":

My father is sleeping. His noble face
suggests a mild heart;
he is so sweet now . . .
if anything bitter is in him, I must be the bitterness.

There is loneliness in the parlor; they are praying;
and there is no news of the children today.
My father wakes, he listens
for the flight into Egypt, the good-bye that dresses wounds.
Now he is so near;
if anything is distant in him, I must be the distance.

And my mother walks past in the orchard,
savoring a taste already without savor.
Now she is so gentle,
so much wing, so much farewell, so much love.

There is loneliness in the parlor with no sound,
no news, no greenness, no childhood.
And if something is broken this afternoon,
and if something descends or creaks,
it is two old roads, curving and white.
Down them my heart is walking on foot.[14]

Of Vallejo, Wright has said, simply, "He draws strength from every
kind of reverence," a strength Wright himself seems to value above all
others. The poem, from Vallejo's first book, *The Black Riders*, shows
great restraint, clarity of tone, and so much tenderness in the distance
of memory evoked by the always-ongoing present tense, the "now" of
dream time. It is a homecoming poem, yet the home is without news,
or sounds; it is the idea of home only, a healing of wounds in imagi-
nation that the poem registers as its immense sadness.[15] The speaker
resigns himself to his responsibility and is reduced to the sound of
his retreating footsteps.

The parallels suggest that Wright may have had this poem in mind
when he was at work on one of his lovely later poems about home:
"Two Postures Beside a Fire," from *Shall We Gather at the River* (1968):

Tonight I watch my father's hair,
As he sits dreaming near his stove.
Knowing my feather of despair,
He sent me an owl's plume for love,
Lest I know not, so I've come home.
Tonight Ohio, where I once
Hounded and cursed my loneliness,
Shows me my father, who broke stones,
Wrestled and mastered great machines
And rests, shadowing his lovely face.

2

Nobly his hands fold together in his repose.
He is proud of me, believing
I have done strong things among men and become a man
Of place among men of place in the large cities.
I will not awaken him.
I have come alone, without wife or child
To delight him. Awake, solitary and welcome,
I too sit near his stove, the lines
Of an ugly age scarring my face, and my hands
Twitch nervously about.

Like the Vallejo poem, "Two Postures" is a homecoming poem with a similar dreamlike present-tense tableau, a kind of ritual celebration of the nobility of the human form in repose with the quiet and restraint of a chapel service. For Wright it is a dream of a sort of reconciliation with home and Ohio, of the proud acceptance of the burden of life that *is* life. But, again like Vallejo, it is a reconciliation in imagination only that ends with the speaker's restlessness—his hands neither resting nor turning to work.

"Two Postures" is a clear example of Wright's affiliation with these poets—of homage, even. It is a practice that Wright made part of his poems from the earliest days of his reading Rilke, and Heine and Vogelweide. He translated in order to read these poems; he read them in order to absorb them; he absorbed them into the process of reshaping his own work.

Another example of the intersection of his translation work with his own poems is Wright's poem, "The Jewel," a much admired and anthologized seven-line poem from *The Branch Will Not Break*. In a journal entry from the spring of 1959 the poet writes:

> I am going like a house on fire on the translation of Trakl. He didn't make sense before—except in his sounds and occasional images—but it has developed that my prolonged and intensive study of Spanish, not to mention my tenacious readings in García Lorca, Vallejo, and Jiménez has taught me how to read Trakl—and also even more important, how to translate him.[16]

By 1959 Wright was immersed in both Trakl and Vallejo, and their work appears side by side in his notebooks of the period along with his own poems. Wright's biographer, Jonathan Blunk, notes the migration of lines from the poet's translation of Vallejo's "Espergesia" that with a few changes and the addition of two new lines would become "The Jewel," "an ideal example of Wright's new style."[17] Blunk continues by quoting a letter from Robert Bly following Wright's death: "I've never known any man who was closer in his inner despair and inner courage to Vallejo than James was. Vallejo made him aware that it was not wrong to try to go deep, even when you found down there immense grief and injustice. And I think Vallejo suggested the value of 'free verse' for that descent."[18]

In "Beyond the Deep Image: James Wright's Vallejo and the Ethics of Translation" (2006), Peter Ramos closely examines Vallejo's importance to Wright's developing "new style" as it appeared in *The Branch Will Not Break*. He points to the poet's practice as a translator, which shows him seeking not to carry over Vallejo's language into his own language, but to discover "forms adequate to the task [that] must echo the strangeness one encounters in reading Vallejo in the original."[19] Indeed, Wright himself has said, "If you try to translate [the poems], you are forced to find some equivalents in your own language, not only equivalents in language itself but equivalents of imagination."[20]

In other words, in the translation process, he finds not only his own language is changed, but also the very ways and means of his own imagination. This was the crucial thing.

Pages from Wright's notebooks and folders from 1960 show him at work on "Espergesia," originally published as "Have You Anything to Say in Your Defense?" by Sixties Press (1963) in *Twenty Poems of César Vallejo*. See page 153. Also shown are two notebook pages from March and April 1962, with versions of "The Jewel" and its tentative placement in *The Blessing*, as *The Branch Will Not Break* was known then.

In 1961 he would publish, with Robert Bly, *Twenty Poems of Georg Trakl*. And in 1971 he chose five among these to include in the "Some Translations" section of his *Collected Poems*. Trakl's poems are difficult, fragmentary, multi-faceted; there is something about them that seems to resist interpretation. Yet as Wright explains, in his "Note on Trakl": "I believe that patience is the clue to the understanding of Trakl's poems. One does not so much read them as explore them." But he also finds a patience in Trakl's stillness, his own willingness to listen, to observe, to wait—without, as Keats says, "any irritable reaching after fact and reason"—as images coalesce and wait for "the inward bodies of things to emerge, for the inward voices to whisper."[21] These inward voices, though, tend outward, too, like Whitman's, or Vallejo's, or Neruda's, toward a world of loneliness, of suffering, of dark indifference. Here is a selection of lines from the Trakl selection in "Some Translations":

from "Trumpets"

Under the trimmed willows, where brown children are playing
And leaves tumbling, the trumpets blow. A quaking of
    cemeteries.
Banners of scarlet rattle through a sadness of maple trees,
Riders along rye-fields, empty mills.

ESPERGESIA (translated from the Spanish of Cesar Vallejo)

fem sing. "Declaración de una sentencia." From Enciclopedia del Idioma,

Vol. II, 1a ed. Martín Alonso Madrid; Aguilar, 1958,

I was born on a day
when God was sick.

They all know that I am alive,
that I am vicious; and they don't know
the December of my birth from today's January.
Well, I was born on a day
when God was sick.

There is this cave
in the air behind my body,
that nobody is going to touch:
this small room of silences
that spoke to a flower of fire.

I was born on a day
when God was sick.

Brother, listen to me, listen...
Oh, all right. Don't worry; I won't leave
without taking my Decembers,
without leaving my Januaries behind.
Well, I was born on a day
when God was sick.

They all know that I am alive,
that I chew my food... and they don't know
why my verses are full of such harsh scrapings:
~~the slight problem of changing position in the darkness~~
of a coffin, and the scratching of winds
that have to be untangled by the Sphinx, → *die*
who interviews the desert.

Yes, they all ~~know~~ ... Well, they don't know
that the light gets skinny
and the darkness gets bloated...
and they don't know ~~that~~ the light and ~~shadow~~ are joined *shadow*
by a Mystery, a hunchback
musical and sad, who stands a little way off and ~~damns~~ *curses.*
the noon for walking beyond its proper boundaries. *[trespassing.]*

I was born on a day
when God was sick,
gravely.

                         --from Los Heraldos Negros (1918)

Passing of verdict, or judgment.

4.2   A notebook page from August 14, 1960, showing Wright at work on "Espergesia," first published as "Have You Anything to Say in Your Defense?" in *Twenty Poems of César Vallejo.*

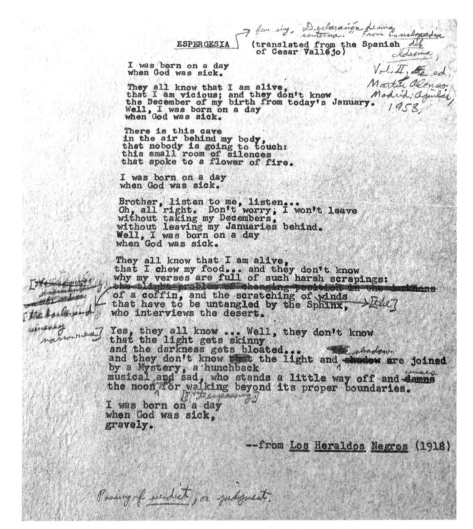

ESPERGESIA (translated from the Spanish
of Cesar Vallejo)

I was born on a day
when God was sick.

They all know that I am alive,
that I am vicious; and they don't know
the December of my birth from today's January.
Well, I was born on a day
when God was sick.

There is this cave
in the air behind my body,
that nobody is going to touch:
this small room of silences
that spoke to a flower of fire.

I was born on a day
when God was sick.

Brother, listen to me, listen...
Oh, all right. Don't worry, I won't leave
without taking my Decembers,
without leaving my Januaries behind.
Well, I was born on a day
when God was sick.

They all know that I am alive,
that I chew my food... and they don't know
why my verses are full of such harsh scrapings:
the slight problem of changing position in the darkness
of a coffin, and the scratching of winds
that have to be untangled by the Sphinx,
who interviews the desert.

Yes, they all know ... Well, they don't know
that the light gets skinny
and the darkness gets bloated...
and they don't know that the light and shadow are joined
by a Mystery, a hunchback
musical and sad, who stands a little way off and damns
the noon for walking beyond its proper boundaries.

I was born on a day
when God was sick,
gravely.

                                        --from Los Heraldos Negros (1918)

4.3 A typescript from Wright's black translations folder showing "Espergesia" close to its
published form. Note stanza 3's transition into Wright's poem "The Jewel," later published
with two added lines in *The Branch Will Not Break*.

Four: Leaves after Winter

Black violets. Flayed birds. Defeated days.
Even their bones lie colorless at last.
I sacked an apple tree, I loved a face.
They flare so richly, they fall gray so fast.

```
There is this cave
In the air behind my body
That no one is going to touch,
A cloister, a silence
Closing around a blossom of fire.
As I stand upright in the ████████ wind,
My bones are dark emeralds.
```

Note (March 18, 1962):

add the following to the mss. of *The Blessing*:

1. Anacreon's Grave
2. In the Cold House
3. Arriving in the Country Again
4. Trying to Pray
5. The Presences of the Dead in Avenues
6. A Prayer to Escape from the Market Place
7. Mary Bly
8. Spring Images
9. "There is this Cave"

4.4   An early version of "The Jewel," with a list of potential additions to the manuscript of *The Blessing*, one of many working titles for *The Branch Will Not Break*. First in that list is Wright's translation of Goethe's "Anacreon's Grave," which he omitted from the book.

4.5 Another early version of "The Jewel" from his 1962 notebook. Wright will shorten line 6 significantly for the published version.

from "De Profundis"

It is a stubble field, where black rain is falling.
It is a brown tree, that stands alone.
It is a hissing wind, that encircles empty houses.
How melancholy the evening is.

Beyond the village,
The soft orphan garners the sparse ears of corn.
Her eyes graze, round and golden, in the twilight
And her womb awaits the heavenly bridegroom.

On the way home
The shepherd found the sweet body
Decayed in a bush of thorns

from "A Winter Night"

With a stiff walk, you tramp along the railroad embankment with huge eyes, like a soldier charging a machinegun nest. Onward!

Bitter snow and moon.

A red wolf, that an angel is strangling. Your trouser legs rustle, as you walk, like blue ice, and a smile full of suffering and pride petrifies your face, and your forehead is white before the ripe desire of the frost;

The lines have a sculptural quality, like an abstract landscape. In a letter Trakl describes his method this way: "my pictorial manner forges together four separate image-parts in four lines of a stanza into a single impression."[22] The effect is similar to Whitman's catalog inasmuch as it proceeds by a kind of parallelism, without subordination or conjunction, in the way it gives priority to seeing/observing, before knowing and making and writing. The tense is a continuous present, a dreamlike, always ongoing-ness; the impression is of an underlying sadness, yearning and emptiness. Although the method may suppress the narrative, we see figures in the landscape, isolated and menaced and ultimately abandoned.

Something of the same parallelism, quiet observation, and underlying sadness can be seen in Wright's own "Twilights" from *The Branch Will Not Break*:

The big stones of the cistern behind the barn
Are soaked in whitewash.
My grandmother's face is a small maple leaf
Pressed in a secret box.
Locusts are climbing down into the dark green crevices
Of my childhood. Latches click softly in the trees. Your hair is
     gray.

The arbors of the cities are withered.
Far off, the shopping centers empty and darken.

A red shadow of steel mills.

Feb. 6, 1960:

TWILIGHTS

free

~~In the cathedral of bees,~~
~~A cicada sheers, crying, down.~~

And the arbors of the cities are withered.
Somewhere, far off,
The shopping centers empty and darken.

A red shadow of steel mills.

***

Twilights (March 31, 1960)

The big stones of the cistern behind the barn
are soaked in whitewash.
My grandmother's face is a small maple leaf
Pressed in a secret ~~folded~~ box.
~~Locusts are complaining all over Ohio.~~
~~Keep your hands to~~ climbing down into
Locusts are ~~complaining all over~~ the dark green crevices
Of my childhood. Latches click softly in the trees. Your hair is gray.
And the arbors of the cities are withered,
Somewhere, far off,
The shopping centers empty and darken.
~~Into~~ red shadow of steel mills.

4.6   A typescript dated February 6 and March 31, 1960, with Wright's lovely poem "Twilights" in its nearly final form.

Here it's as if the images are chiming off of each other: the big stones/a small maple leaf; my grandmother's face/your hair, searching for a melody, building a song, but not a story; a secret box/the cistern behind the barn/shopping centers/steel mills. The lines each present different images, as if entering and leaving a series of rooms—"the latches click softly in the trees." But the poem's movement is of color and scale and light, of the open and the closed, of the proximate and the far-off—one kind of twilight for the childhood world, another kind for the withering cities with the garish light of their mills.

While thinking through implications of form, order, surface, and depth, Wright may have, in fact, also been reworking Rilke in his mind. He undoubtedly knew Rilke's "The Archaic Torso of Apollo," from *Neue Gedichte* (1908), and he worked feverishly at dozens of Rilke translations in the 1940s and 1950s. In "Archaic Torso," Rilke writes a manifesto on intellect and intuition, on the manifest and the hidden:

> We cannot know his legendary head
> with eyes like ripening fruit. And yet his torso
> is still suffused with brilliance from inside,
> like a lamp, in which his gaze, now turned to low,
> gleams in all its power . . .[23]

This is a poem about what we cannot know, yet through the art of it, through the relation of its materials, its shapes, we can feel the source of its power.[24] This "brilliance from inside" confuses us at the same time it shows us what Whitman called "the path between reality and the soul." With Rilke, Wright has come to a confidence that the path of his perceptions and intuitions, rather than the point-to-point ordering of argument, is the sure way to the true inward clarity of the soul.

Wright was at special pains to describe in detail what he meant by Whitman's "delicacy," and it has an important connection back to just this inner brilliance ("innigkeit") that Rilke describes:

> Whitman's poetry has a delicacy of music, of diction, and of form. The word "delicacy" can do without a rhetorically formal definition; but I mean to suggest powers of restraint, clarity, and wholeness, all of which taken together embody that deep spiritual inwardness, that fertile strength, which I take to be the most beautiful power of Whitman's poetry.[25]

In the end, Wright's restlessness, his candor and courage, his constant artistic exploration were matters of this deep spiritual inwardness. In a lovely letter to the editor Michael Cuddihy praising the work of poet and translator H. R. Hays (September 15, 1979), Wright observes that "there is a difficult nobility in poetry which commands, or ought to command, our whole spiritual attention."[26] This nobility, a nobility which is difficult, suggests an art that will require everything.

5. Here Is Nourishment: The Spanish Poets

ANNE WRIGHT

Although James Wright was familiar with the work of many poets who wrote in the Spanish language, his first center of interest was in translating poetry written in German. In fact, when he received his first copy of *The Fifties*, he was most excited by Robert Bly's interest in the work of Georg Trakl. He felt that no one on the Minnesota faculty knew of this poet. This lack of interest, plus the condescension showed toward Walt Whitman, had depressed him. He read and reread *The Fifties*, feeling at last there was a publication with editors who reflected his own beliefs about poetry.

James carried out a voluminous correspondence with Bly and took many trips to the Bly farm.

His first trip there, with his wife Lib and their two sons, was a successful and happy visit. In James's thank you note he wrote: "please forgive the slight delay in acknowledging your hospitality to us . . . We all retain sensations of luminous space and kindness. I myself feel as the ripening orchard must have felt in the moonlight of late summer."[1]

The moonlight of that late summer visit was to frequently shine. Weekend after weekend James would arrive, usually alone, after a three-hour bus trip, with a briefcase bulging with work and just a few clothes. Robert's love and interest in the work of poets writing in Spanish was infectious, and soon James was as involved as Robert. The two poets spent long hours reading, discussing, and working on the poetry of Lorca, Neruda, Vallejo, and Jiménez, among others.

During that time of frequent visits to the farm in the late fifties, James wrote about these translations in his journal and in letters, particularly those to a young writer for whom he was both teacher and mentor. His life in Minneapolis had become extremely difficult. The farm was both a refuge from deeply serious problems and a place where he was respected and his presence affectionately enjoyed. Carol and Robert gave him incredible support and friendship. The translations gave him stimulation, an expanded view of poetry, and influences for his own work.

Although he had studied Spanish in high school at Martins Ferry, Ohio, he had turned to an extensive study of German while an undergraduate at Kenyon College. A Fulbright year in Vienna had strengthened his facility to speak and write in German. A few months after his first visit to the farm he noted in his journal, dated October 26, 1958, that he bought a book on Spanish grammar.

At the same time, James's life in Minneapolis continued to be difficult and dark. He had arranged a study in the basement of his tiny house where, as he wrote to Donald Hall, he could work "with the furnace, the moths, the skeletons of mice and the necklaces of twilight."[2] The peace of the basement study and frequent trips to the Bly farm were his salvation.

In a letter to Robert and Carol from March 1959, he writes just how much the translation work and this new direction for his own poetry means to him: "I cling patiently to the South Americans and other translations, partly because they are life and death to the thing in me that wanted and needed to be a poet in the first place."[3]

In a letter from April 10, 1959, Robert Bly writes: "Thank you for the translations of Vallejo and Neruda. I was so inspired by them that I sat up late last night planning a series of five books for *The Fifties* to publish . . ."

The excerpts that follow are from the poet's personal journal entries—many written at a table in two Minneapolis coffee shops of the day, The Golden Gopher and Gopherland. Also included is a series of unpublished letters to a "young writer" (recalling Rilke's *Letters to a Young Poet*), and letters to the Blys and others from February 1959 to November 1960.[4] All are transcriptions from originals

Monday.

Dear Jim,

I think a separation was wise. I know it is very hard for both of you now, and probably harder for h..? than for you, because she is a woman and has a mother's worries, but "what is fated cannot be fled, and what cannot be avoided must be borne."

Work hard and think without malice.

No one can understand another marriage, so I must leave it. There, with affection and respect.

Thank you for the translations of Vallejo and Trakl, and Neruda. I was so inspired by them that I sat up late last night planning a series of five books for the Fifties to publish:

Twenty Poems of Pablo Neruda, translated by Irene Rathburg, Robert Bly, and James Wright

Twenty Poems of Cesar Vallejo - translated by James Wright

Twenty Poems of Georg Trakl. translated by James Wright and

Ten Poems of René Char; translated by Robert Bly

Forty Poems of Juan Ramón Jiménez - translated by ...

5.1 Letter from Robert Bly to Wright, April 1959: "Thank you for the translations of Vallejo and Trakl, and Neruda. I was so inspired by them that I sat up late last night planning a series of five books . . ."

collected in the James Wright papers in the Upper Midwest Literary Archives (UMLA) at the University of Minnesota, some of which have since been published in *A Wild Perfection: The Selected Letters of James Wright* (Farrar, Straus and Giroux, 2005).

JOURNAL ENTRY, DATED FEBRUARY 19, 1959

(Still morning, reading Jiménez for my health)

I can't afford to buy the complete works of Jiménez and yet I need them so terribly, the way a man needs water.—that I will proceed slowly but regularly to copy 5 poems each morning into my commonplace book. This will take a long time but I must go on living and here is nourishment.

The following is from one of Wright's letters "to a young writer," this one dated February 22, 1959:

I will write out for you a single one of the greatest lyrics by Lorca, and then give you as good a translation as I can, side by side and line by line. Now it will probably be helpful to you (for you will be as unaccustomed to the Spanish imagery, the way of conveying a meaning through images and nothing else, as I have been) if I tell you a detail. Lorca's poem is called "Malagueña," which is simply the name of a kind of Spanish dance, or perhaps a certain kind of tune which is played on a guitar. Okay—now, you must understand that this poem tries to tell what the tune on the guitar creates in the mind of the poet as he hears it. That is, the poem's truth is subjective. (But it is still truth!)

La muerte	Death
entra y sale	enters and leaves
de la taberna	in the tavern
Pasan caballos negros	Black horses
y gente siniestra	and sinister men
por los hondos caminos	pass on the deep roads
de la guitarra.	of the guitar.

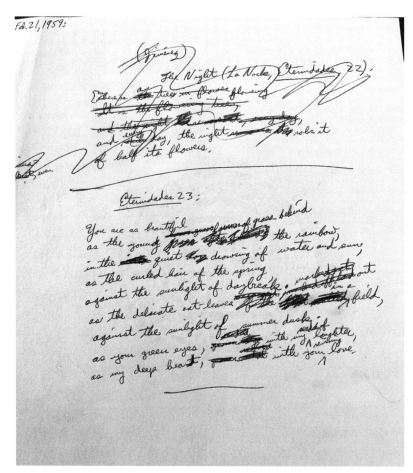

5.2 A draft of Wright's translation of Juan Ramón Jiménez's "You Are as Beautiful," February 21, 1959. See Wright's comments on page 113.

Y hay un olor a sal	And there is an odor of salt
y a sangre de hembra	and of the blood of a woman
en los nardos febriles	in the feverish roses
de la marina	of the sea.
La muerte	Death
entra y sale	enters and leaves,
y sale y entra	and leaves and enters,
la muerte	death
de la taberna	in the tavern

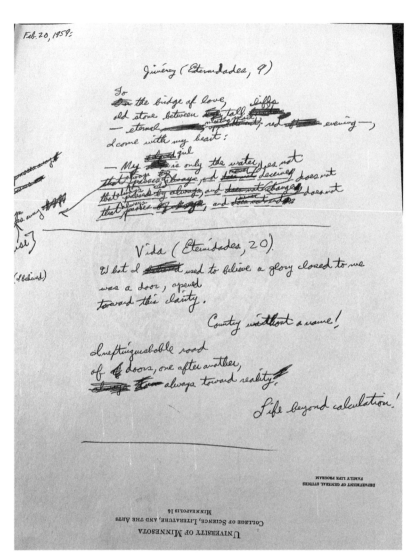

5.3 Early drafts of Wright's translations of Jiménez's "To the Bridge of Love" and "Life."

Oh, if only I could learn it. They have dropped all the rhetoric and gone straight to the truth of the soul itself and insisted that the heart _is_ true, that we have <u>no right</u> to reason it away, and they can drop the rhetoric (which I have so often used as a mere defense against experience) because they are not afraid.

But I'm not afraid either! I just realized it again—I'm not afraid.

There is one other thing which has kept me alive during the past terrible days—one other thing and that is Spanish poetry. Here are a couple of the gorgeous, reviving, happy poems of Jiménez that I have clung to in the middle of hell. He is such a great, noble human being . . . loving, and kind and tender and joyous in the midst of pain. Here are 2 poems I've translated from his book *Eternidades* (Eternities)

You are as beautiful
as the young lawn behind the rainbow,
in the quietness of drowsing water and sun;
as the curled hair of spring,
against the sunlight of dawn;
as the frail oat-plants marked out in a field,
against the sunlight of a dusk in summer;
beautiful as your green eyes,
with my grained laughter;
beautiful as my deep heart,
with your reviving love.

LIFE

What I used to regard as a glory shut in my face
was a door, opened
towards clarity:
    Country without a name!
Nothing can destroy it, this road
of doors, opening one after another,
always toward reality:
    Life without calculation!

Well, for years I have loved Whitman in secret. If I mentioned him, and the meaning of his art, I was sneered at. So I bided my time.

And now, just at the moment when I was absolutely alone and could not hide from my own soul's duty to itself any more, I discovered what has happened to the tradition of Whitman. It is alive to the south of us.

. . . Now look at any issue of, say *The New Yorker*; and look at the verses you see printed there. You will find them all neat, secure, comfortable, clever, safe, and not one line in ten thousand could possibly make you give a damn whether you live or die. Then compare those cunning, clever, little verses which we write in the United States today with the following translation of a poem which I just made. It is by a Peruvian poet, César Vallejo. And it is called "The Eternal Dice."

Here is an early version of the translation published in *Twenty Poems of César Vallejo* (Sixties Press, 1962). See page 155 in the "Selected Spanish Translations" section of this book for the published version.

THE ETERNAL DICE

My God, I am weeping for the life that I live,
it is hard to grasp at your bread;
but this thinking, starving piece of mud
is not a leavened crust at your side:
he can't escape into your Mary-candles.

My God, if you could have been man,
you would have wanted to be God;
but you, who were always well,
feel nothing of your own creation.
And if man suffers—he is God!

Today there are candles in my broken eyes,
as in the eyes of a condemned man;
my God, put lights in your windows,
and we will gamble with the old, worn-out dice.

Sometimes, oh gambler! to show how lucky
The whole universe is,
The snake-eyes of the dead, circled with worry, turn up,
Two funeral aces of slime.

My God, in this blind and deafened night,
you can't play anymore, because the earth
has already been tossed and rounded by pure chance,
and it can't make itself stop in vacancy,
in this vacancy of enormous sepulchre.

I do not intend to live the rest of my life writing respectable little
verses which are really an evasion of the grandeur and terror of
life. Like Thoreau "I am determined not to live what is not life,
living is so dear."

A copy of the same poem, slightly revised, was enclosed in a letter to
the same recipient on March 16, 1959, to which he appended this note:

I made the above translation. It is, I believe nearly the most
successful one I have made so far, although I have one from
Pablo Neruda (the poem is called "No Hay"—which I translate
as simply "I Can't Forget") and Neruda is lovely, not so ecstatic
and mystical and violent as the Vallejo poem above. Still, the
Neruda is sad, so I will keep it back for a bit.

FROM A LETTER TO A YOUNG WRITER, DATED
    APRIL 8, 1959

Today I was miserable and I got working on the gorgeous poet
Vallejo again (he's the one from Peru) and I have completed two
translations from him which I think are somewhat successful.
Anyway, the poems seemed to me so utterly beautiful . . .

The poem's first twelve lines are included here. The complete text—
slightly revised—is included on page 157 in the "Selected Spanish
Translations" section of this book.

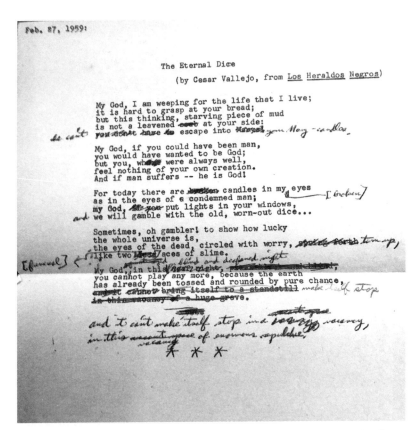

5.4   An early draft from February 27, 1959, of Wright's translation of Vallejo's "The Eternal Dice."

THE BIG PEOPLE
   (A child speaks in this poem)

What time are the big people
going to get back.
Blind Santiago is striking six
and already it is dark.

Mother said she wouldn't be delayed.

Aguedita, Nativa, Miguel,
Be careful of going over there, where
doubled-up griefs, whimpering their memories,
have just gone

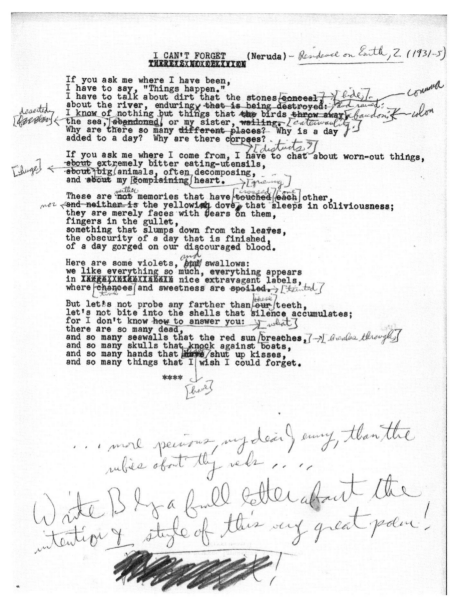

I CAN'T FORGET   (Neruda) – *Residence on Earth, 2 (1931-5)*

If you ask me where I have been,
I have to say, "Things happen."
I have to talk about dirt that the stones conceal,
about the river, enduring that is being destroyed:
I know of nothing but things that the birds throw away,
the sea, abandoned, or my sister, wailing.
Why are there so many different places? Why is a day
added to a day? Why are there corpses?

If you ask me where I come from, I have to chat about worn-out things,
about extremely bitter eating-utensils,
about big animals, often decomposing,
and about my complaining heart.

These are not memories that have touched each other,
and neither is the yellowish dove that sleeps in obliviousness;
they are merely faces with tears on them,
fingers in the gullet,
something that slumps down from the leaves,
the obscurity of a day that is finished,
of a day gorged on our discouraged blood.

Here are some violets, and swallows:
we like everything so much, everything appears
in nice extravagant labels,
where chances and sweetness are spoiled.

But let's not probe any farther than our teeth,
let's not bite into the shells that silence accumulates;
for I don't know how to answer you:
there are so many dead,
and so many seawalls that the red sun breaches,
and so many skulls that knock against boats,
and so many hands that shut up kisses,
and so many things that I wish I could forget.

****

5.5 March 1959 draft of Wright's translation of Neruda's "No Hay Olvido (Sonata)," entitled "I Can't Forget." Below the typescript, he wrote: "Write Bly a full letter about the intention & style of this very great poem!" and a quote from Sterne's *Tristram Shandy* about fleeting time: ". . . more precious, my dear Jenny, than the rubies about thy neck . . ." (the name Jenny appears in many Wright poems).

toward the quiet poultry-yard, where
the hens are still being settled,
they have been startled so much.

BLACK STONE UPON A WHITE STONE

I shall die in Paris, of rain,
on a day which I already remember.
I shall die in Paris—I am not running—
on some Thursday, like today, in autumn.

It will be Thursday, because today is Thursday,
And it makes verses prosaic, and the smoke-flues
Have made me sick, and, as never before, I have turned
with the road, to see myself walking, alone.

César Vallejo died, stricken down by the very things
Without which he would have built up nothing;
They toughened him with a club; they toughened him
with a rope also; and there are witnesses—
the days called Thursday, the storm flues
the solitude, the falling of rain, the roads.

Wright's translation of "Black Stone upon a White Stone" was never
published. A different version was published in *Neruda and Vallejo:
Selected Poems.*

You know he actually did die on Thursday (in 1938), alone, in
a charity hospital, in Paris, and it was raining, and he had tu-
berculosis, and he suffered malnutrition, and he was wounded
in the trenches during the Spanish Civil War, and he was all
prepared, through help of friends, to return to his native Peru
and recover, and he was informed that the Loyalist Armies in
Spain had been defeated and were retreating from Caledonia
and he grew so angry at the inhumanity of it that he died, and
he was forty years old, and he was a very great and brave man,
and he never successfully found his love either, and many peo-

ple no doubt would have made him ashamed of being kind of wild and silly, an emotional cripple, but he faced his conditions of suffering, and he did not quit, and his collected poems are three hundred pages long, and he won, no matter what the world did, no matter that he failed to find his real love, and I owe him so much, because he reminded me that perhaps I too might somehow vindicate myself, not only as an artist but even as a human being.

A revision of his own "Spring Images" was the journal entry dated April 13, 1959. This appeared in *The Branch Will Not Break* in a slightly altered form.

SPRING IMAGES

Two athletes
Are dancing in the cathedral
Of the wind.
A butterfly lights on the branch
Of your green voice.
Antelopes
Are sleeping in the ashes of the moon.

A page from Wright's notebook from 1959 shows an even earlier draft of "Spring Images" with three other short poems. Both versions here differ from the one eventually published in *The Branch Will Not Break*. A fourth, "Shame," is canceled with the comment: "Too close to Vallejo's" written in the margin. The line in Spanish below the draft is from one of Vallejo's poems in *Trilce*, "Oh the Four Walls of the Cell," which Wright translated and published in *Chelsea* 7 (May 1960). The complete translation is included on page 148 in the "Selected Spanish Translations" section.

JOURNAL ENTRY, DATED APRIL 14, 1959

I am going like a house on fire on the translation of Trakl. He didn't make sense before—except in his sounds and occasional

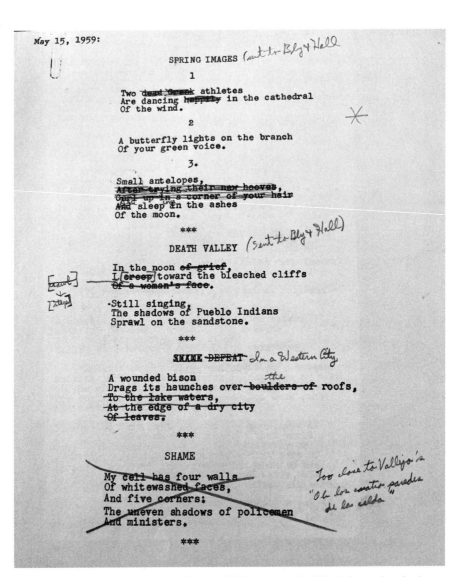

5.6 Early draft of Wright's "Spring Images," May 15, 1959. See Wright's note beside the crossed-out "Shame": "Too close to Vallejo's 'Oh las cuatro de la celda'."

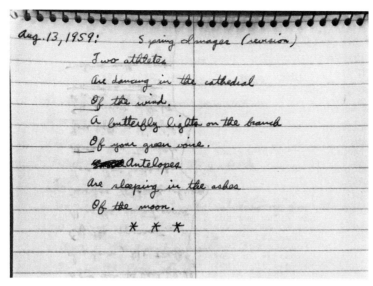

Aug. 13, 1959:   Spring Images (revision)

Two athletes
Are dancing in the cathedral
Of the wind.
A butterfly lights on the branch
Of your green voice.
~~The~~ Antelopes
Are sleeping in the ashes
Of the moon.
    * * *

5.7   A later version of "Spring Images," from a notebook entry dated August 13, 1959.

images—but it has developed that my prolonged and intensive study of Spanish, not to mention my tenacious readings in García Lorca, Vallejo, and Jiménez has taught me how to read Trakl—and also even more important, how to translate him.

FROM A LETTER TO JAMES DICKEY,
    DATED APRIL 17, 1959

I do know that for the past two weeks, heaven knows why, I have started to write again. And I am getting adroit as hell in reading Spanish. I have discovered the great Peruvian poet César Vallejo, and man he is one of the great ones. Here is one of the ten poems that I have translated.

What follows is an earlier draft. The complete text as published is included on page 155 in chapter 6, "Selected Spanish Translations."

OUR DAILY BREAD

Breakfast is drunk down . . . damp earth
of the cemetery freezes the precious blood.

Nourishment: The Spanish Poets   121

City of winter . . . the biting crusade
of a wheelbarrow appears, hauling
an emotion of fasting in chains.

I wish I could beat on all the doors,
and ask for somebody; and then,
look at the poor and, while they wept softly,
give bits of fresh bread to all of them
And plunder the rich of the vineyards
with my two blessed hands
which, with one blow of light,
could blast nails from the cross.

Eyelashes of morning, Thou wilt not rise!
Give us our daily bread,
Lord . . . !

Every bone in me belongs to others
and maybe I robbed them.
I came to take something for myself that by chance
was meant for another;
and I think that, if I had not been born,
another poor man might have drunk this coffee!
I feel like a dirty sneak-thief . . . Wherever I go!

And in this cold hour, when the earth
transcends human dust and is so sorrowful,
I wish I could beat on all the doors,
and beg pardon from someone,
and make bits of fresh bread with it
here, in the oven of my heart.

FROM A LETTER TO A YOUNG WRITER,
    DATED APRIL 22, 1959

I wanted to write also to tell you—I know I'll get it all confused,
I just can't convey it, I guess—how profoundly thrilled and joy-
ful I am over what is taking shape in me. It is the first big step in

the major literary effort of my life. Did I tell you that an editor-friend of mine has pretty well made publishing arrangements for my next book? This one will be an interim affair, for it will consist of translations, but the poet I'm translating is so great, so huge, so humane and original! And I feel as if great doors were opening in me all the time. One of the ten Jiménez translations that I sent you (all ten to be in a forthcoming anthology) describes most amazingly well what I feel about the current project that I'm working on: an image of great doors opening and one doesn't know what exactly is on the other side, and one is apprehensive and frightened, and the doors open on glory.

LIFE

What I used to regard as a glory shut in my face
Was a door, opening
Always towards this clarity:
                Country without a name.

Nothing can destroy it, this road
Of doors, opening, one after another,
Always toward reality:
                Life without calculation!

Anyway, my book of translations will be called *Twenty Poems of César Vallejo*, translated by J.A.W.

While most of the translations in *Twenty Poems of César Vallejo* were translated by James alone, several were written in conjunction with Robert Bly and John Knoepfle.

JOURNAL ENTRY DATED APRIL 23, 1959

A . . . great German is Eduard Mörike, who is hard to translate. And Goethe! My God, no matter what anyone says about his pompousness, his lyricism in his youth is incomparable! I have no copy of German lyrics in the office at the moment, and I will rely on memory for something or other. Let me see, now. Oh, yes:

Dem Schnee, dem Regen	Against snow, rain
Den Sturm entgegen . . .	storm, (I move)
soll ich fliehen	But shall I flee it,
Wälderwärts ziehen?	Flee into the woods?
Alles vergebens,	That does no good!
Krone des lebens	Crown of life,
Glueck ohne Ruh!,	Happiness without rest,
Liebe, bist du!	Love art thou.

When one loves a thing, one has got to realize that a struggle of devotion will be involved. It is a thrilling poem; though, once again, I made it sound like hell in English.

Ah, but is Goethe's line in *Faust*, when the hero says to the passing moment of time, "Verweile doch! Du bist so schoen." It is one of the greatest moments of human triumph through language over mortality, that line; and it can be pretty well rendered in English thus: "Linger awhile, thou art so fair." Isn't that lovely?

Poets of this kind can be a consolation all your own. One of the places where you can completely retire alone, for the refreshment of your spirit through the sharing of your pathos with kindred spirits who will not pooh-pooh the very real truth of your feeling but who, since they also know what you feel can speak to you in private about that feeling, can help you shape it and give it meaning within yourself and yet respect the feeling, and respect you have for it.

The following schedule for work appears here in the notebook.

JOURNAL ENTRY, DATED APRIL 1959

Going through proofs of *Saint Judas*
Plans to translate Guillén's *Cántico*

Work on lecture about Nietzsche
Translate Neruda's "Sexual Water" with Robert
Translate for Vallejo
Own work

This entry was started on April 24 and finished on April 26.

FROM A LETTER TO ROBERT BLY,
DATED APRIL 26, 1959

I received your letter on Friday, and just simply and flatly dropped every "busy" job I had to do as if I were a snake shedding its old skin (the spring is gorgeous!). I took Neruda and two dictionaries and a scratch-pad and then walked all over the place: along the river, all over the campus, up and down this street and that alleyway and so on; and here is the translation. I think it is done. I had two very intelligent friends go over the English with me. I know I've got the Spanish correct. Well, all I can say is that I think it is done.

. . . working on Neruda's masterful poem gave me a wonderful weekend of joy; and I needed that, as you can imagine. I feel like a green thing, growing.

Although there is no copy of the translation sent with this letter, it is likely that the Neruda translation that James sent was "Sexual Water."

In the section of his memoir called "Living in Machado," Phil Levine recalled a meeting with the Spanish critic, editor, and translator Hardie St. Martin, who had just embarked on his groundbreaking anthology of Spanish poetry in English translation, *Roots and Wings.* Levine writes: "He had already enlisted the cooperation of Kinnell, Merwin, Haines, Stafford, Wright and Bly. He asked me if I were interested in contributing, and I assured him I was, although as yet my Spanish was almost non-existent. It didn't matter, he remarked, Bly couldn't order a glass of water in Spanish, but he had a genius for translating the poetry."[5]

I now have fourteen poems of Vallejo translated; a few in nearly final form, most in sketches which are grammatically correct but still rough in the rhythm and syntax of their English.

When some 25 of them are completed I will send them all to Robert for criticism and suggestions.

It seems to me that there should be four different groups: one dealing with Vallejo's love of home; one dealing with his poverty and compassion for the sufferers of big cities; one dealing with his surrealistic exploration of himself and one dealing with the war.

It is intensely difficult to grasp Vallejo's dangerous and wildly ranging yet precise new style. Whenever I work on his poems I feel the little used ligaments of my imagination stretching. So much the better. For Vallejo often reveals to me things about myself which I hadn't known or even suspected. And these things are joyous and—oddly—unafraid.

JOURNAL ENTRY, DATED MAY 25, 1959

Today I did a little translating, and I think I have nearly completed a good version of Vallejo's "Los Pasos de Janos." I will return to it later, but first, of course, it must be allowed to ripen. The same is true of the poem (from *Trilce*) that deals with the woman who is constantly seeking Vallejo in her hand, but they are separated by a cat, a basin of tepid water and by time. These poems are powerfully moving in Spanish. I hope I can catch more of them in English.

JOURNAL ENTRY, DATED MAY 27, 1959

Yesterday I did complete a translation of Guillén's great lyric "Quiero Dormir" and the labor strengthened me a little.

FROM A LETTER TO A YOUNG WRITER, DATED JUNE 2, 1959

Recently I found two poems by my favorite César Vallejo of Peru, poems about his home, and I wanted to send them to you (in my own translations) because I felt you would like them. They are all tenderness and kindness.

The first of them is a lament for his dead brother, and the second is a dream of his parents.

You will notice that in both poems Vallejo returns home, and the place seems empty somehow even though mother and father are there—yet they are ghostly, and the poet is ghostly, and I find the whole thing hauntingly beautiful. I hope you like them. You must let me know how they strike you. Okay?

What follows is an early draft. The complete text of the poem as published is included on page 154 in chapter 6, "Selected Spanish Translations."

TO MY BROTHER MIGUEL

Brother, today I sit on the brick bench
of the house,
       where you make a bottomless emptiness.
I remember we used to play at this hour and
Mama
Caressed us: "But, sons . . ."

Now I hide
       As before, from her evening
       lectures, and I trust you not to give me away.
Through the parlor, the vestibule, the corridors.
Later, you hide, and I do not give you away.
I remember, we made ourselves weep,
brother, in that game.

```
            (from the Spanish of Cesar Vallejo)

                To My Brother Miguel

                   in memoriam

        Brother, today I sit on the brick bench of the house,
        where you make a bottomless emptiness.
        I remember we used to play at this hour, and mama
        caressed us: "But, sons..."

        Now I go hide
        as before, from all not evening
        lectures, and I trust you not to give me away.
        Through the parlor, the vestibule, the corridors.
 [later]←Afterwards, you hide, and I do not give you away. (I remember we laughed till
        I remember we made ourselves weep,                    we cried)
        brother, in that game.
                                                  chuckling
        Miguel, you went into hiding              [      ]
        one night in August, toward dawn,
        but, instead of laughing in concealment, you were sad.
        And the twin heart of those dead evenings
 grew  became annoyed at not finding you. And even yet now
        a shadow falls on my soul.

        Listen, My brother, don't be late
        coming out. All right? Mama might worry.
                   ***         --from Los Heraldos Negros
```

sent to Bly

~~Brother~~ *Remember we made ourselves cry*
Brother, from so much longing.

5.8   In a June 2, 1959, letter to "A Young Writer," Wright refers to "two poems by my favorite César Vallejo of Peru, poems about his home . . . They are all tenderness and kindness."

The Vallejo continues. I have found an absolutely breathtaking poem about the death of his brother. Wait till you see it. I swear, translating him is beyond question the most beautiful experience in writing that I have ever had in my life. I think often that, in spite of how much the rest of life seems to be falling into little pieces, it is such a relief that I have come to find joy in writing poetry again.

The text of "The Distant Footsteps" as it appears in *Twenty Poems of César Vallejo* and in *Neruda and Vallejo: Selected Poems* is included on page 94 in chapter 4.

I want to enclose two new translations for you . . . I am thinking in particular of the one called "The Garden Within." The poems are translated from the Spanish of an old and great man named Jorge Guillén . . . Guillén has lived in the U.S. for the past twenty years and now his great book, *Cántico*, is being published in a bilingual edition in NYC by Gaetano Massa, a brilliant Puerto Rican book seller. To get back to "The Garden Within," I knew you would be interested; for in his poem Guillén describes the beautiful garden of safety and happiness, a kind of Eden which we all seek; and then harsh reality breaks in, and the poet asks where the <u>Garden</u>, itself a greater reality and not a dream, has gone. And he answers that the garden remains "within"—within us.

The poem's first three stanzas are included here. The complete text is included on page 172 in chapter 6.

For Emilio
warm and chiseled clarity
Gabriel Miró

Flat roofs, turrets, domes
Approximate the desires
Of the streets and public squares
For their heaven.

Holiday.
Clouds, clouds of amusement!
Slow, unattached, they
Shift, wander without a goal.

A luminous circle.
A city blurred from within,
May, unhastening toward June
Abandons itself to its own interval.

The following translation of "Everyone's Hope" was published in *Jorge Guillén's* Cántico: *A Selection*, edited by Norman Thomas di Giovanni (Boston, Little Brown & Co., 1965).

EVERYONE'S HOPE

Everyone's hope!
And everyone with the sun and morning
Gathered into a murmur,
Into a smile of luster,
Into a praise that moves, delighting itself,
From the people to the cloud,
From the balcony to the iridescent foam,
Fused with the oar in a polish
Of festival.
The disturbance of the sun
Continually stirs ambling feet

That crawl after the passers-by
In expectation and hope.
Where is this hope?
Boys help one another into the trees
And grow there, among the leaves,
Gratings, joyous in profile,
Still adolescent
A beginning warmth, an early warmth
Of a spring wholly shared,
Announces
The lucky vastness of the summer.
On the widespread murmur, the cry passes
To the distance, dissolving
Bland cry of no one for no one.
If nothing impedes it, joy comes, floating
Smoothing the discords to satin.
The uproar of fiesta,
Of warmth that is friend,
Of crowds like groves
Under the sun the multitude flashing
With laughter and gazes,
So many that they lose their way
Among so many crossroads
Of light, sap, and the multitude that searches.
Hope! Everyone's hope!
A compass, a parade
Invocation, exclamation, praises,
—nothing more worthy of praise—
And the green river that passes, nearly
Reddish, if not rich brown,
The river that encloses,
Likewise,
From bridge to bridge under the spring,
The great civil stream of history.
Where is hope?
The multitude crowds toward the brightness,

Hindering one another, to a flood tide
That they greet like a sign, a gift
Of summer to come.
Harnesses, spangles, velvets
Of triumph!
The brave hope
Thrusts inward, scatters,
Beautiful, general:
A people, a gathered people, exercising
A health that is shared,
A health like a festive gift,
Lake an extravagance that delights itself.
And upon the sidewalks,
Colorful clouds move past.
And the towers, the towers hung
With plain April in blossom,
The towers after centuries
—without pride—beautiful for everyone.
Where, finally, where?
They gather to search now, festive,
To search for hope.
Oh virgin hope, so divine,
So embraced by the air,
And by the silence of the moments.
There are many
In spite of a pacified rumor,
Many above the peace
Of men,
Turning back to their hope
Of April.
And the blood flows through their bodies
Active, owing no sacrifice,
Blood for this hope.
How deep this hour, like morning,
Happiness decorated
With the plain truth of spring!

And lives cross one another,
High, radiant lives.
Under the azure, suddenly—silence?
A cheer. Hurrah! The sudden ovation
For pure convergence in the sun.
A chorus? No. Better:
Common April on a solitary earth,
April!
All at once it is possible
To grow rich in joy for the mere sun
Of so much forgetful joy,
For the stirring accumulation
Of clarity and hope.
In the air, a future
Free, free from death
—or with life in death, farther on.
Expectation of endless life
For me, for everyone.
An open path to the hours!
I shout to the sun, the flood, the plain of fiesta.
The multitude surges in its gaiety,
And all things are united again,
Fertile.
Everyone's hope!

FROM A LETTER TO ROBERT AND CAROL BLY,
DATED OCTOBER 29, 1959

. . . I don't know. The best thing about Guillén, for me, is that sketching English versions of his short poems is simply like reading him—just simply reading a poet. It seems so long since I have done that, I had forgotten how much it meant.

He enclosed translations of two Guillén poems with this letter, "The Snow" and "The Shadow," which are published here for the first time on pages 171 and 172 in chapter 6.

I want to write at this moment and say I too am delighted—that isn't the word for it—over the Trakl translations. Just a little while ago I went over them and to do this after leaving them alone for a few days is to see how they really do sound—and look, and feel—like Trakl's own poems . . .

I received the translations today when I felt terribly depressed, and they lifted my spirits . . .

At the moment I am awfully pushed by affairs at school. So much work to be done continually. But somehow—God, literally, God knows how—I am going to hang on, to the translations at the moment and to other poems when they return. It is really very much like a man fallen overboard, clinging helplessly and yet by pure subconscious instinct to a rope whose other end is held by somebody he can't even see, on the other side of a cloud of fog.

I enclose once more, stages of Vallejo. They speak for themselves. Please go over them when you can. It occurred to me this morning again that Vallejo has poems of different kinds—different kinds of images and different kinds of situations—and we might consider arranging them this way. For example he has several love-poems written about prostitutes. In this kind of poem, he is almost always walking alone in the rain in some city, Paris or Lima and remembering the girl. I've been working recently on one poem of this kind. It's called "Poema Para ser leído y cantado," and I made the following entry into my journal. There are 5 whore-poems of this kind—the thing that V. is always deeply involved, as a male and as a human being, with the professional lovers whom he picks up—and he seems to carry the smallest details about them—their slight, unconscious and yet uniquely *characteristic* gestures of the hands or feet—in his imagination wherever he goes . . . It is crucially important to translate these strange love-poems *without* any tough-talk, any slang of the kind that some recent idiotic translators of Catullus have used, in short without any implicit denial of tenderness. i.e. the diction in V's poems to and about whores is delicate and respectful to them, as women and as human beings. Vallejo says *Thou* to prostitutes. Society considers whores inhuman. Even the whores themselves agree and they talk tough. What V's diction reflects is his tacit assumption that whores are women. It is a very revolutionary idea. This ripple of male tenderness is what we must capture in English. And so on.

Thank you so much for the Trakl. It meant more to me than I can describe, especially today. In a moment I must go upstairs for the evening meal. Do you remember Sisyphus in hell, forever pushing the enormous boulder up the slope, getting to the top, slipping and having it fall down again, again, and again and again, forever? In a moment I must go up to the evening meal.

FROM A LETTER TO ROBERT AND CAROL BLY,
DATED MAY 11, 1960

I'm enclosing 2 little poems, 2 versions of the one and the finished version of the other. I am really astonished at the Hernández poem—how it emerged. I have been trying to get at it—reach the poem, I mean, the poem is still hiding, rather frightened, behind the rhetoric . . . I think in these new poems I am still afraid myself and all those little animals sense my fear, and all they do is wait for a long, long time, with their eyes every once in a while looking out between the leaves to see if I've grown patient and trusting enough to let them come out without putting them in a cage and sending them immediately to *The Partisan Review*.

I'll close for now. I like to think of both of you, right this moment, sitting outside on the porch or maybe walking toward the barn. I wish I could hear an owl tonight.

I spent a lot of time this afternoon on the epigraph of Lorca's "Tarde" poem:

(Estaba mi Lucia
con los pies en el arroyo?)

Was my Lucia
standing (or walking) in the stream?

or

Was that my Lucia,
with her feet dangling in the water?

or

Was my Lucia
dangling her feet in the stream?

For the full text of "Tarde" ("Afternoon"), see page 147. Wright's September 7 letter to Robert Bly continues:

An arroyo is a stream-bed. But the dictionary doesn't help much. Frankly, I'm afraid of the thing. Why not just omit the epigraph, both Spanish and English? I don't think it would show any disrespect to Lorca to do so, and besides, your point as I get it is to show how he could just write a little poem about "Afternoon" by waiting patiently for it to fill up with little images, like that "gauze painted with little green moons." The epigraph sounds awfully personal and obscure.

I also think the Trakl translation looks fine. I look forward to your introduction as soon as it arrives. I'll finish mine and speed it back to you . . . I think the 20 poems will make it an extremely beautiful book. And I'm convinced we were right in waiting so long over those poems. They ripen into meaning for us . . . I think our translation has profited a great deal by our doing it slowly. Because we had no model to go by . . . [Wright's ellipses] that's just the point. We were like Lewis and Clark, tracing our delicate strange places inside Trakl, all alone without anything from the past to guide us. His poems are there and our translations are like encampments from which we make excursions in among the trees and sudden clearings, and make notes while we interview those odd beautiful little animals in there. So the delay was a ripening. There is a sentence in Meister Eckhart which comes to mind: "God will make up for all time lost for His sake."

I've been going over the Ohio poems, and they get shorter and shorter, and I think better. I also wrote one about Pine Island which I'll send you soon.

Another thought occurred to me; do you think it would be worthwhile to quote D. MacDonald's short passage about Whitman, Baudelaire etc. "turning their faces away from the marketplace?" For, you know, poets in America get hypnotized into fearing that, if they turn away from the market, they won't be poets anymore. It is stupid, but very powerful, and has to be shaken off, among other soporifics.

FROM A LETTER TO W. D. SNODGRASS,

    DATED NOVEMBER 17, 1960

Twice now you've asked about my translations and new poems. The new poems are sometimes crazier than hell. What else? They are still not good enough. What else?

Well, it is now 11:00 p.m. I got back a little bit ago and typed up three things: one translation from César Vallejo of Peru and two new poems of my own. There are a bunch of short, weird ones but I haven't got that notebook with me here. I don't know about these things. They may be imprecise and too vaguely wild, God damn it, but they don't have to be. Vallejo isn't. And I don't think we have yet had a poet in the states who can come even

2:30 A.M.
Tues., March 23, 1965

Recently I found a little notebook which I used during late Spring and early Summer of 1962. In my relations with the world, that was a pretty dark period, to put it mildly. And yet — I am astonished at my little notebook of 1962. Here it lies before me now — in fact, I am writing these words on one of its unmarked pages — triumphantly, clear, orderly, neat, and, in its own way, shining.

It also happens to contain several completed poems of that year; and three of them were printed in my book The Branch. How very strange! At that time I was — in relation to the world, to "others" (whoever they may be, those strangers amongst whom I have crept, crouched over like a stone in the rain, for more than thirty weary, wearying years), defeated, smashed, scarred.

And yet, there is my little notebook. On April 30, 1962, I suddenly wrote "The Jewel"; and it appears in The Branch with very slight changes. Also on April 30, 1962 — there it is, right on the next sheet in this very notebook — I wrote, straight out in longhand, without the slightest correction even in ink or punctuation,

5.9   A notebook entry from March 23, 1965, in which Wright describes himself as "astonished" by the discovery of a pocket notebook from 1962, when he was "defeated, smashed, scarred."

close near the clarity and precision of Machado and Jiménez. Well, that's hysterical, but you know what I mean.

FROM A LETTER TO E. L. DOCTOROW, DATED MARCH 13, 1964

. . . The chance to work on the Storm translations was, more than once, the chance to go on living

. . . Edgar, I want to thank you and the others for giving me a chance to work on this translation. Never once was it a burden. It was always, rather, a source of nourishment and re-freshment; and the completion of the book is the fulfillment of an old dream of mine.

JOURNAL ENTRY, DATED MARCH 17, 1965

Recently I found a little notebook which I used during late spring and early summer of 1962.

In my relation to the world that was a pretty dark period to put it mildly. And yet—I am astonished at my little notebook of 1962. Here it lies before me now—in fact I am writing these words in one of its unmarked pages—triumphantly clear, or-derly, neat and, in its own way, shining.

It also happens to contain several completed poems of that year; and three of them printed in my book *The Branch*. How very strange. At that time I was—in relation to the world and "others" (whoever they may be, those strangers amongst whom I crept, crouched over like a stone in the rain, for more than thirty weary, wearying years), defeated, smashed, scarred.

And yet, there is my little notebook. On April 30, 1962 I sud-denly wrote "The Jewel" and it appears in *The Branch* with very slight changes. Also, on April 30, 1962, there is, right on the next sheet in this very notebook—I wrote straight out in longhand, without the slightest correction even in ink or punctuation, a little poem I decline to name because I know, if I know any-thing—it is incomparably the truest and best thing I was ever blessedly lucky enough to write. Then, a couple of pages further,

I find three versions of "To the Evening Star" which, like the other two was later printed in *The Branch*.

I believe the poem that he "declined to name" is "Beginning."
Of the notebook, Wright continues:

I suppose the notebook with its poems wasn't enough to save, much less justify, my life—my solitary and (as always) incommunicable disaster. But my little notebook was all I had. Edward Thomas, whose writings I love beyond those of any other author in any language, writes these words concerning a tramp (hobo) with whom he once traveled some distance on foot.

> The stars in their courses were
> not more serene, more lonely, than he.
> Such a friend of night was he, the stars
> were nearer to him than man. "If only
> they would warm my hands," he cried.
>
> But of course they would not and will
> not, and I am he.[6]

6. Selected Spanish Translations by James Wright

In James Wright's first reference to translating a poem from Spanish, in a letter dated February 22, 1955, he writes, "I will write out for you a single one of the greatest lyrics by Lorca, and then give you as good a translation as I can . . ." He went on to draft dozens of Spanish translations and publish more than fifty poems by Spanish-language poets throughout the 1960s. (See the Selected Bibliography.) The selection included here represents four groups: 1) translations discussed in the preceding text; 2) published versions of earlier drafts of translations quoted in the text; 3) translations published in journals, but uncollected; and 4) translations never published that were discovered among the poet's papers at the University of Minnesota's Upper Midwest Literary Archives (UMLA).

Citations and publication history are given at the end of the book in the Sources for Translations.

Anne Wright

JUAN RAMÓN JIMÉNEZ (1881–1958)

from *Diario XXXVI*, February 4, 1916

SKIES

One sky each day,
each night . . .

Hollow pursuing hands
that trust the sea for a moment.

But I, a mere child, escape day
after day, night
after night,
like a butterfly.

FEDERICO GARCÍA LORCA (1898–1936)

from *Libro de Poemas*, 1921

AIR OF NIGHT

I am very afraid
of the dead leaves,
afraid of the meadows
filled with dew.
I'm going to sleep;
if you do not waken me,
take my cold heart to your side.

Who is this, making sounds
very far off?
Love. The wind in the glass windows,
my love!

Pierce your necklaces
with jewels of the dawn.
Why do you abandon me
on this road?
If you go very far away,
my bird weeps
and the green vineyard
will not yield its wine.

Who is this, making sounds
very far off?
Love. The wind in the glass windows,
my love!

Who is this, making sounds
very far off?
Love. The wind in the glass windows,
my love!

ANOTHER DREAM

A swallow flies away
toward the far distance . . .

There are flowery shapes of dew
upon my sleep,
and my heart turns round and round,
filled with boredom,
like a merry-go-round where Death
goes riding with her small children.
I wish I could fasten Time
into these trees
with a cable of black night,
and paint on it with my blood
the pale shores
of my memories.
How many sons does Death have?
They are all in my breast!

A swallow comes back
from the far distance.

DREAM

I went, mounted upon
a male goat.
The grandfather spoke
and said to me: "This is your pathway."
"This!" cried my shadow
disguised as a beggar.
"That golden one!" said
my clothing.
A huge swan winked at me,

saying, "Come with me."
And a serpent nibbled
my coarse traveling garment.

Gazing at heaven, I thought:
"I have no pathway.
The roses of the end will be
like those of the beginning.
The flesh and the dew may be
changed into the mist."

My fantastic horse carried me
over a reddish countryside.
"Let me go!" I cried, weeping,
to my pensive heart.
I abandoned it in the earth,
filled with sorrow.
               The night came,
filled with wrinkles
and shadows.
            And the road lit my way,
and the luminous and bluish eyes
of my male goat.

from *Canciones*, 1927

AUGUST

August.
The opposing
of peaches and sugar,
and the sun inside of the afternoon,
like the stone in the fruit.

      The ear of corn keeps
its laughter intact, yellow and firm.

      August.

The little boys eat
brown bread and rich moon.

JUAN BREVE

Juan Breve
had a giant's body
and the voice of a small girl.
Nothing like his trill.
Singing, he was
the very pain
in the back of a smile.
He calls up the groves of lemon trees
in sleeping Malaga,
and his lament carries the flavors
of the salt of the sea.
Like Homer, he sang
blind. His voice
held something of the sea without light,
sweetness of oranges.

LAMENTATION FOR THE DEAD

On the black sky,
yellow serpents of stars.

I came into the world with eyes,
and I see without them.
Master of the larger pain.
Presently,
a brass lamp and a coarse cotton blanket
on the ground.

I wanted to come to the place
where gentle men come.
And I have arrived, my God! . . .
But presently,
a brass lamp and a coarse cotton blanket
on the ground.

Little yellow lemon tree,
lemon tree.
Toss your small lemons
to the wind.
You know, all of you! . . . Because, presently,
a brass lamp and a coarse cotton blanket
on the ground.

On the black sky,
Yellow serpents of stars.

SEA

The sea is
the Lucifer of azure.
The sky fallen
in the desire to be light.

Poor sea, condemned
to eternal movement,
having before been quiet
in heaven.

But love would ease you
of your bitterness.
Give birth to pure Venus,
And your depth would stay
virgin, barren of pain.

Your sadnesses are beautiful women,
sea of glorious spasms.
But today, instead of stars,
you contain pulps of green.

Endure your suffering,
formidable Satan.
Christ walked upon you,
but so did Pan your son.

Venus the star is
the harmony of the world.
Let the clergy be silent!
Venus is the profound
of the soul . . .

And miserable man
is an angel, fallen,
and the earth our probable
ruined paradise.

AFTERNOON

Was my Lucia standing
with her feet in the river?

    Three immense poplars
And one star.

    The silence, nibbled
By the frogs, resembles
A painted gauze
With small green blemishes.

    In the river,
A dry tree
Has shed blossoms,
Widening the circles.

    Sounding over the waters
To the tawny girls of Granada.

CÉSAR VALLEJO (1892–1938)

Three poems from *Trilce*, 1922

I AM FREED

when the waters come towards me.

We are always scattering salt.

We season the marvelous song, the good-luck song
on the lower lips of desire.
Oh beautiful virginity.
The saltless breeze passes.

From the distance, I breathe marrows,
Hearing the profound score, as the surf
hunts for the keys.

And if we spoke this way of the nostrils
in the absurd,
we should cover our poverty with gold,
and hatch the still unborn wing
of the night, sister
of the orphaned wing of the day,
that is not really a wing, being alone.

TORMENTED FUGITIVE, COME IN, GO OUT

On the same quadrangular forge.
Doubt. The balance pierces and pierces
Up to the hilt.

Sometimes I give in to all enemies,
and for a while I am the blackest of high peaks
in the accidental death of harmony.
Then my dark eyes are divinely irritated,
and the mountain range of my soul begins sobbing,
oxygen forces itself, delighted,
flaming, up and down, until
grief doubles up its peak with laughter.

But one day you will not be able to come
nor to leave, when I fling a handful of earth
into your eyes, fugitive!

OH THE FOUR WALLS OF THE CELL

Ah the four white walls,
they can't help it, they always come out four.

6.1 An early draft of Vallejo's "*Trilce* XVIII."

Greenhouse of nerves, painful opening:
in the four corners they are always uprooted,
the arms and legs that are chained every day.

Loving woman, keeper of numberless keys,
if you were here, if you could just see
how the hours are these four walls.
We should lean on them together, the two of us,

we two more than ever. And you would not weep,
I swear, my saviour!

Ah the four walls of the cell.
Yet I pity the walls, and mostly, tonight,
those two long ones that hold
some shape of mothers who carry
the dead down the slopes of bromide,
each one holding a little boy by the hand.

And I alone draw to one side, left back
holding up my right hand, that serves for both hands,
in search of a third arm
that will have to house, between my where and my when,
this sickly majority of men.

AT THE BORDER OF A FLOWERING GRAVE

At the border of a flowering grave,
two marys go into the past, weeping,
weeping whole seas.

The ostrich stripped of its memory
stretches out its last feather,
and with it the denying hand of Peter
carves on Palm Sunday
resonances of funeral services and stones.

From the border of a stirred-up grave
two marys drift away, singing.

Monday.

IN THAT CORNER WHERE WE SLEPT TOGETHER

In that corner where we slept together
so many nights, I've sat down now
to take a walk. The bedstead of the dead lovers
has been taken away, or what could have happened.

You came early for other things,
But you're gone now. This is the corner
where I read one night, by your side,
between your tender breasts,
a story by Daudet. It is the corner
we loved. Don't confuse it with any other.

I've started to think about those days
of summer gone, with you entering and leaving,
little and fed up, pale through the rooms.

On this rainy night,
already far from both of us, all at once I jump . . .
There are two doors, swinging open, shut,
two doors in the wind, back, and forth,
shadow   to   shadow.

from *Los Heraldos Negros*, 1919

CHALK

Silence. It is already night here,
the sun gone behind the cemetery,
and a thousand eyes go on weeping:
you do not come back; already my heart is dead.
Silence. Everything here is still dressed
in stiff mourning; and my passion
scarcely burns, it is like weak kerosene.

Spring will come. You will sing "Eva"
after a minute that lies down, after a
furnace where fragrant sexual oils are burning.
Try to forge pardon for the poet down there,
because I have been full of grief
ever since the nail fastened the coffin!

More . . . one night of poetry, your
kind breast, your red sea

will be stormed upon, with the waves of fifteen years
and you will see, far off, laden with memories,
my dark boat of criminals, my ingratitude.

Then, your apple orchard, your yielding lips,
let blossoms fall on me for the last time;
they died bleeding with so much love
like a pagan figure of Jesus.

Love, you will sing;
and make the woman in my soul shiver
as in a darkened cathedral.

POEM TO BE READ AND SUNG

      I know there is someone
looking for me day and night inside her hand,
and coming upon me, each moment, in her shoes.
Doesn't she know the night is buried
with spurs behind the kitchen?

      I know there is someone composed of my pieces,
whom I complete when my waist
goes galloping on her precise little stone.
Doesn't she know that money once out for her likeness
never returns to her trunk?

      I know the day,
but the sun has escaped from me;
I know the universal act she performed in her bed
with some other woman's bravery and warm water, whose
shallow recurrence is mine.
Is it possible this being is so small
even her own feet walk on her that way?

      A cat is the border between us two,
right there beside her bowl of water.
I see her on the corners, her dress—once

an inquiring palm tree—opens and closes. . . .
What can she do but change her style of weeping?

But she does look and look for me. This is a real story!

HAVE YOU ANYTHING TO SAY IN YOUR DEFENSE?
(ESPERGESIA)

Well, on the day I was born,
God was sick.

They all know that I'm alive,
that I'm vicious; and they don't know
the December that follows from that January.
Well, on the day I was born,
God was sick.

There is an empty place
in my metaphysical shape
that no one can reach:
a cloister of silence
that spoke with the fire of its voice muffled.

On the day I was born,
God was sick.

Brother, listen to me, Listen . . .
Oh, all right. Don't worry, I won't leave
without taking my Decembers along
without leaving my Januaries behind.
Well, on the day I was born,
God was sick.

They all know that I'm alive,
that I chew my food . . . and they don't know
why harsh winds whistle in my poems,
the narrow uneasiness of a coffin,
winds untangled from the Sphinx
who holds the desert for routine questioning.

Yes, they all know . . . Well, they don't know
that the light gets skinny
and the darkness gets bloated . . .
and they don't know that the Mystery joins things together . . .
that he is the hunchback
musical and sad who stands a little way off and foretells
the dazzling progression from the limits to the Limits.

On the day I was born,
God was sick,
gravely.

TO MY BROTHER MIGUEL

in memoriam

Brother, today I sit on the brick bench outside the house,
where you make a bottomless emptiness.
I remember we used to play at this hour of the day, and mama
would calm us: "There now, boys . . ."

Now I go hide as before, from all these evening prayers,
and I hope that you will not find me.
In the parlor, the entrance hall, the corridors.
Later, you hide, and I do not find you.
I remember we made each other cry,
brother, in that game.

Miguel, you hid yourself
one night in August, nearly at daybreak,
but instead of laughing when you hid, you were sad.
And your other heart of those dead afternoons
is tired of looking and not finding you. And now
shadows fall on the soul.

Listen, brother, don't be too late
coming out. All right? Mama might worry.

THE ETERNAL DICE

for Manuel González Prada, this wild and unique
feeling—one of those emotions which the great master
has admired most in my work

God of mine, I am weeping for the life that I live;
I am sorry that I have stolen your bread;
but this wretched, thinking piece of clay
is not a crust formed in your side:
you have no Marys that abandon you!

My God, if you had been man,
today you would know how to be God,
but you always lived so well,
that now you feel nothing of your own creation.
And the man who suffers you: he is God!

Today, when there are candles in my witchlike eyes,
as in the eyes of a condemned man,
God of mine, you will light all your lamps,
and we will play with the old dice . . .
Gambler, when the whole universe, perhaps,
is thrown down,
the circled eyes of Death will turn up,
like two final aces of clay.

My God, in this muffled, dark night,
you can't play anymore, because the Earth
is already a die nicked and rounded
from rolling by chance;
and it can stop only in a hollow place,
in the hollow of the enormous grave.

OUR DAILY BREAD

for Alejandro Gamboa

Breakfast is drunk down . . . Damp earth
of the cemetery gives off the fragrance of the precious blood.

Vallejo, Our Daily Bread (from Los Heraldos Negros

~~They drink their breakfast~~... Damp earth
Breakfast is drunk (absorbed, consumed) upon...
of the cemetery freezes the precious blood.
City of winter... the biting crusade
of a wheelbarrow appears, hauling
an emotion of fastings in chains.

I ~~would have liked to~~ ~~XXXXXXXXXXXXXXXXXX~~
wish I could
beat ~~XXXXX~~ ~~at~~ all doors,
and ask for somebody; and then,
~~to~~ look at the poor, and, while they wept softly,
~~to~~ give bits of fresh bread ~~to them~~ *all of them,*
And ~~to~~ plunder the rich of their vineyards
with my two blessed hands
which, with one blow of light,
could blast nails from the Cross!

Eyelash of morning, Thou wilt not rise!
Give us our daily bread,
Lord...!
Every bone in me belongs to others
~~My very bones belong to others;~~
and ~~perhaps I stole them.~~
maybe I robbed them.

I came to take something for myself that by chance
was meant for ~~XXXXX~~ another;
and I think that, if I had not been born,
another poor man could have drunk this coffee!
I feel like a dirty sneak-thief... Wherever I go!

And in this ~~cold~~ hour, when the earth
frigid
~~passes beyond~~ human dust and is so sorrowful,
I wish I could beat on all the doors,
and beg pardon from someone,
and make bits of fresh bread ~~XX~~ with it
here, in the oven of my heart...!

***

Sent to Bly (yes)
(not for Fifties)

6.2   An early draft of Vallejo's "El Pan Nuestro," translated as "Our Daily Bread."

City of winter . . . The mordant crusade
of a cart that seems to pull behind it
an emotion of fasting that cannot get free!

I wish I could beat on all the doors,
and ask for somebody; and then
look at the poor, and, while they wept softly,
give bits of fresh bread to them.
And plunder the rich of their vineyards

with those two blessed hands
which blasted the nails with one blow of light,
and flew away from the Cross!

Eyelash of morning, you cannot lift yourselves!
Give us our daily bread,
Lord . . . !

Every bone in me belongs to others;
and maybe I robbed them.
I came to take something for myself that maybe
was meant for some other man;
And I start thinking that, if I had not been born,
another poor man could have drunk this coffee.
I feel like a dirty thief . . . where will I end?

And in this frigid hour, when the earth
has the odor of human dust and is so sad,
I wish I could beat on all the doors
and beg pardon from someone,
and make bits of fresh bread for him
here, in the oven of my heart. . . !

WHAT TIME ARE THE BIG PEOPLE COMING BACK?

What time are the big people
going to come back?
Blind Santiago is striking six
and already it's very dark.

Mother said that she wouldn't be delayed.

Aguedita, Nativa, Miguel
be careful of going over there, where
doubled-up griefs whimpering their memories
have just gone
toward the quiet poultry-yard, where
the hens are still getting settled,
who have been startled so much.

"The ~~Older~~ Big People"

~~[crossed out]~~ ...at what time are the big people
going to come back?
Blind Santiago ~~strikes~~ six, → is striking
and already it is ~~totally~~ very dark.
Mother said she wouldn't ~~be~~ be delayed.
Aguedita, Nativa, Miguel,
be careful of going over there, where
doubled-up griefs whimpering their memories
have just gone ~~now~~
toward the quiet poultry-yard, where
the ~~hens~~ are still being settled,
they have begun ~~to~~ started so much.
We'd better ~~leave~~ just stay ~~by~~ here.
Mother said that she wouldn't be delayed.
And we shouldn't be sorry. Let's go see
the boats — mine is ~~prettier than~~ ~~the~~ anybody's! —
we were playing ~~them~~ the whole blessed day,
without ~~fighting~~ ~~among ourselves~~, ~~just~~ as it ~~must~~ be:
they stayed in the puddle of water, all ready ~~too~~,
loaded ~~up~~ with pleasant things for ~~tomorrow~~.
Let's wait this way ~~[crossed out]~~, obedient ~~to~~
and helpless, for the homecoming, the apologies
of the big people ~~who~~ who are always the first
to abandon the rest of us in the house, —
as if we ~~too~~ couldn't ~~escape~~ get away too,
Aguedita, Nativa, Miguel?
I am calling, searching blindly [hit-or-miss] in the
Don't leave me ~~[crossed out]~~ behind to look) darkness,
[by myself]

~~[crossed out]~~ the only one locked in.

Pozo or Hudson?

S... H. Mrs.

6.3   An early draft of César Vallejo's "*Trilce* III," "Las personas mayores," trans-
lated by Wright here as "The Big People."

158

We'd better just stay here.
Mother said that she wouldn't be delayed.

And we shouldn't be sad. Let's go see
the boats—mine is prettier than anybody's!—
we were playing with them the whole blessed day,
without fighting among ourselves, as it should be:
they stayed behind in the puddle, all ready,
loaded with pleasant things for tomorrow.

Let's wait like this, obedient
and helpless, for the homecoming, the apologies
of the big people, who are always the first
to abandon the rest of us in the house—
as if we couldn't get away too!

Aguedita, Nativa, Miguel?
I am calling, I'm feeling around for you in the darkness.
Don't leave me behind by myself,
to be locked in all alone.

I STAYED HERE, WARMING THE INK
IN WHICH I DROWN

       I stayed here, warming the ink in which I drown,
and listening to my other cavern,
nights of touch, days of mental drifting.

       Something unknown quivered in my tonsils,
and I creaked with my annual melancholy,
nights of sunlight, days of moonlight, sunsets of Paris.

       And yet, even today, at the fall of evening,
I digest the most holy loyalties,
nights of the mother, days of the great-granddaughter,
two-colored, voluptuous, urgent, charming.

       Nevertheless
I do come abreast, I overtake myself in a two-seater airplane,

6.4 An early draft of Wright and Bly's translation of Vallejo's "Quedéme a calentar la tinta en que me ahogo," rendered as "I stay here, warming the ink in which I drown."

under the domestic morning, and the fog
that crept out of a second forever and ever.

     And yet,
even now,
inside the tail of the comet in which I've won
my happy PhD germ,
here I am, burning, listening, masculine-earthlike, sunlike,
masculine-moonlike,
I cross the graveyard unrecognized,
swerve to the left, cutting
the grass with a pair of hendecasyllabics,
years in the sepulcher, liters of infinity,
ink, pen, bricks, and forgivings.

CLAPPING PALMS AND GUITARS

Now, between ourselves, here,
come with me, lead me by the hand to your body
and let us feast together and pass an instant from life
into two lives, giving one part to our death.
Now, come with yourself, do me the kindness
of resting inside my name and the gleam of dark night
where you lead my hand to your soul
and we flee away on small knives from ourselves.

Come to me, and to yourself, yes,
so the two of us can be seen, stepping unevenly,
marking time at farewell.
Until we return! Until that coming back!
Until we can read, though we are ignorant!
Until we return, saying goodbye!

What do rifles matter to me,
listen to me;
listen to me, what do they matter to me,
if the bullet already circles my signature?
What do bullets matter to me,
if the rifle fires already in your fragrance?
Right now let us weigh
our star in the arms of a blind man
and let us weep, both at once, as you sing to me.
Right now, beautiful woman, with your even pace,
with your believing trust that I weep in alarm,
let us balance ourselves, two by two.
Until we are blind!
Until
we weep with so much turning!

Now,
between ourselves, lead me

by the hand into your sweet person
and let us feast together and pass an instant from life
into two lives, giving one part to our death.
        Now, come with yourself, be kind to me,
sing something
and play the instrument in your soul, clapping your palms
until we return! Until then!
Until we are gone, say goodbye!

from *Los Heraldos Negros*, 1919

GUNWALES OF ICE

I come, day after day, to see you passing,
little enchanted fog, always distant . . .
your eyes are two blond captains;
your mouth, a short red sail
that undulates in a farewell of blood.

I come to see you passing; until one day,
intoxicated by time and cruelty,
little enchanted fog, always distant,
the star of evening will break apart.

Riggings; treacherous winds; winds
of woman that passed:
your cold captains will give orders,
and the one who founders shall be myself.

EL ACENTO ME PENDE DEL ZAPATO

My accent trails from my shoe;
I hear it perfectly,
giving way, shining, doubling up, shaped like amber
and dangling, a stain, an unlucky shadow.
It is so much larger than I am,
judges study me from a tree,
they study me, their tails wagging, across the way,
they creep into the bone of my ear,

they put me up to stare at a girl
and, downstairs in the urinal, they shrug their shoulders.

Certainly nobody is walking beside me,
it isn't important, I don't need anything;
certainly, they said I am walking:
yes, that's it.

But that mumbling is the cruelest of all!
Humiliation, glare, deep jungle!
It leans over me, so huge, elastic fog
snapping together above and below me.
They don't make a sound! not a sound! And then, then
the ominous telephones start buzzing.
It's the Accent: he's the one.

From *Trilce*

SO MUCH HAIL THAT I REMEMBER

So much hail that I remember,
And pile on a few pearls
to those I have pulled right from under
the snout of the other storms.

I don't want this rain to dry up.
At least not unless they let me fall
right now instead of it, or unless they buried me
soaked in the water
shooting up from every fire in the world.

I wonder where the water-line on my body will be?
I'm afraid I'll be left with one of my sides dry.
I'm afraid the rain will end before I'm tested
in the bone-dry months of the incredible vocal chords,
where to create harmony
we have to rise always! and never go down!
Well, don't we rise, really, to go down?

Sing on, rain, on this coast still with no sea!

Trilce, # LXXVII

~~SHHH XX XHHHHH XXHHH HHHHH~~   may
~~The hail storms so violently,~~ I/remember
~~It~~ *gather*
and ⌐increase⌐ the pearls *from*
that I have ⌐gathered~~ out of~~ the same mouth
of every tempest. *[harvested]*

This rain is not going to ~~dry~~ away (up).
Unless I ~~might~~ happen *to fall*
~~to fall~~ toward it, or unless they bury me
soaked in ~~the~~ water ~~that~~
that spouts out of all the fires.

Where will this rain carry me?
I am afraid of being left on some dry shore; *tried*
I am afraid the rain is ~~gone~~, without having ~~tested~~
                                 going   me
in the droughts of unbelievable vocal cords,
~~AHHHHX XHHHHX XHHHX~~
~~THHX THHX HHHHX XHX XHHHHX XHHHHHHX~~
those that for the sake
of giving harmony,
are always climbing up, never descending!
Don't we by chance climb in order to find the
          depths?

Sing, rain, on your coast, even if it has no sea!

                    ***

Feb. 29, 60;

There are so many hailstones, I may remember
and gather up the pearls
that I have harvested from the same mouth
of other storms.
This rain is not going to dry away.
Unless I happen to fall
toward it now, or unless they bury me
soaked in that water
that fountains out of every fire.
Where will this rain carry me?
I am afraid of being left on some dry shore;
I am afraid the rain is going away, without giving me a chance
to sing among these droughts of vocal cords that nobody
you believe!
simply for the sake
of making a sound of harmony,

6.5   An early typescript draft with handwritten revisions dated February 29, 1960, of Vallejo's "Graniza tanto, como para que yo recuerde," translated as "So much hail that I remember" and attributed to both Bly and Wright.

164

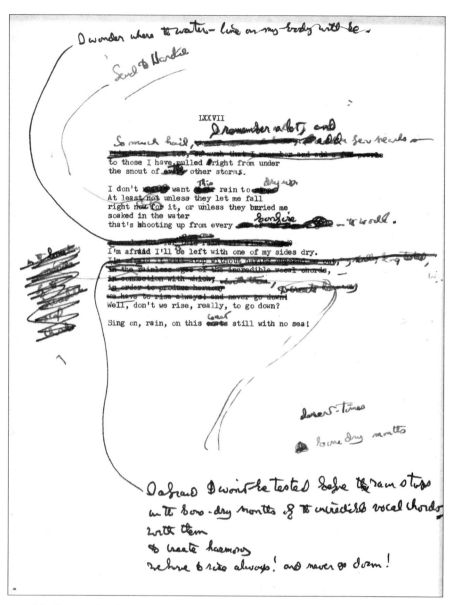

I wonder where the water- lies on my body will be.

Send to Hardie

LXXVII

I remember a lot, and

So much hail, ~~add~~ *few pearls*

~~to those I have~~ *pulled* ~~bright~~ from under
the snout of ~~each~~ other storms.

I don't ~~really~~ want ~~this~~ *the rain* to ~~dry up~~ .
At least not unless they let me fall
right now for it, or unless they buried me
soaked in the water
that's shooting up from every ~~bonfire~~ *in the world* .

I'm afraid I'll be left with one of my sides dry.
~~I'm afraid it will stop without having used me only~~
~~in the painless legs of the incredible vocal chords,~~
~~in connection with which~~
~~in order to produce harmony~~
~~we have to rise always and never go down~~
Well, don't we rise, really, to go down?

Sing on, rain, on this *coast* still with no sea!

loves-times

some dry months

I afraid I won't be tested before the rain stops
in the soo-dry months of the incredible vocal chords
with them
to create harmony
where to rise always! and never go down!

6.6 Much revised and undated draft by Bly of Vallejo's "Graniza tanto, como para que yo recuerde," attributed to Bly and Wright. Bly wrote on this "send to Hardie," referring to Hardie St. Martin, their good friend and frequent collaborator.

PABLO NERUDA (1904–1973)

from *Canto General*, 1950

"IT WAS THE GRAPE'S AUTUMN."

It was the grape's autumn.
The dense vinefield shivered.
The white clusters, half-hidden,
found their mild fingers cold,
and the black grapes were filling
their tiny stout udders
from a round and secret river.
The man of the house, an artisan
with a hawk's face, read to me
the pale earth book
about the darkening days.
His kindliness saw deep into the fruit,
the trunk of the vine, and the work
of the pruning knife, which lets the tree keep
its simple goblet shape.
He talked to his horses
as if to immense boys: behind him
the five cats trailed,
and the dogs of that household,
some arched and slow moving,
others running crazily
under the cold peach trees.
He knew each branch,
each scar on his trees,
and his ancient voice taught me
while it was stroking his horses.

THEY RECEIVE INSTRUCTIONS AGAINST CHILE

But we have to see behind all them, there is something
behind the traitors and the gnawing rats,
an empire which sets the table,

and serves up the nourishment and the bullets.
They want to repeat in you their great success in Greece.
Greek playboys at the banquet, and bullets
for the people in the mountains: we'll have to destroy the flight
of the new Victory of Samothrace, we'll have to hang,
kill, lose men, sink the murderous knife
held to us from New York, we'll have to use fire
to break the spirit of the man who was emerging
in all countries as if born
from the earth that had been splashed with blood.
We have to arm Chiang and the vicious Videla,
give them money for prisons, wings
so they can bomb their own populations, give them
a handout, a few dollars, and they do the rest,
they lie, bribe, dance on the dead bodies
and their first ladies wear the most expensive minks.
The suffering of the people does not matter: copper
executives need this sacrifice: facts are facts:
the generals retire from the army and serve
as vice president of the Chuquicamata Copper Firm,
and in the nitrate works the "Chilean" general
decides with his trailing sword how much the natives
may mention when they ask for a raise in wages.
In this way they decide from above, from the roll of dollars,
in this way the dwarf traitor receives his instructions,
and the generals act as the police force,
and the trunk of the tree of the country rots.

FRIENDS ON THE ROAD (1921)

Then I arrived at the capital, vaguely saturated
with fog and rain. What streets were those?
The garments of 1921 were breeding
in an ugly smell of gas, coffee, and bricks.
I walked among the students without understanding,
pulling the walls inside me, searching
each day into my poor poetry for the branches,

Neruda's FRIENDS ON THE ROAD (1921)

Robert, you'll want to ⬛⬛⬛⬛⬛⬛⬛ re-shape entire
lines and phrases, I imagine. So it's best for you
to just consult the original, for such purposes. I
recall that your impromptu version had some
strikingly beautiful phrases; but I couldn't remember
them when I worked on the poem⬛⬛ yesterday, except
for the first two lines.

However, I think I can help with a couple of
details in my own version, which you should have
by now. Here are my thoughts:

1. In every case, the relative clauses should be
omitted, so the line can be condensed into a
syntax more simple and direct. For example, in
the stanza beginning "I sprouted into life", there
is the line: "filled with hearts that had been
condemned and torn down." Just delete "that had
been.⬛" and notice the effect.
2. The passage in the "I sprouted" stanza that
I've translated as follows:

       The walls became filled with faces:
eyes that did not ⬛⬛⬛ see light, etc......

 I've revised the passage to read as follows:

       The walls filled with faces:
eyes that did not see light, twisted waters
that saw nothing but crime, the outcome
of lonely arrogance, excavations
filled with hearts condemned and torn down.

 ("Excavations" rather than"cavities", because
it's an image of razed hearts in the edge of town,
in the skid road; where we speak of "excavations"
for buildings; "cavities" sounds too much like
bad teeth. (Okay?)

2. In the very last line of the poem, you'll
see that I tried to find a phrase that would
spell out the literal meaning as clearly as
possible. However, it's obvious that part of
Neruda's power of imagination is shown by his
conveying that meaning in only two words,which
are also very concrete (my version has six words,
and they're pretty prosy and abstract). I wish
you would live with that last line for a little
while, and see if you can't meet Neruda at the
peak of his beautiful poem, his beautiful imagin-

6.7 Wright's comments, probably from late 1958, addressed to Bly on
a translation of Neruda's "Compañeros de Viaje": "I wish you would
live with that last line for a little while, and see if you can't meet Ner-
uda at the peak of his beautiful poem, his beautiful imagination."

    the drops of rain, and the moon, that had been lost.
    I went deep into it for help, sinking
    each evening into its waters, grasping
    energies I could not touch, the seagulls of a deserted sea,
    until I closed my eyes and was shipwrecked in the middle
    of my own body.

ation. I'm perfectly confident you can, and I think I've supplied a fairly sturdy groundwork in my literal rendering of the last line.

3. In the very last stanza, I've tentatively revised a passage as follows:

I entered into my human being
singing among flames, given refuge
by companions of the night's own kind,
who sang to me in the taverns,
and spoke to me of tenderness,
and, even more, of a Spring sheltered
by their hostile hands....

That's all that occurs to me right now. I should add only that I think the title FRIENDS ON THE ROAD I is the best of the two which you suggested (your other one was COMPANIONS ON THE ROAD, I think). "Friends" is a very resonant word in our language. In spite of its use to fit special occasions (the Society of Friends, Ingemar Johannsen's "friend", etc.), it has such deep truth of feeling in it that it is still whole and strong, uninjured. Not like "comrade."

I felt so happy yesterday afternoon, reading Neruda's poem, gaining for the first time some really clearer and deeper understanding of the man's nobility; and remembering how much strength we all felt when the Trakl book arrived, and how we did exactly the right thing with that strength (we ploughed it back into the imagination: I mean I do really believe that we worked so well on Neruda, in part at least, because we were so heartened by the arrival of the Trakl); I really felt like rejoicing, and that was why I was so delighted at your phone call and asked X you to talk on for a moment longer.

I won't take time at the moment to type from my journal my notes on prose in general, on your own prose, on your new poems, and on Issa and Basho. I'll do that later. The main point, however, is simply this: those Japanese wrote travel books of prose as settings for their poems. It is a new form for us. You ought to try it, Robert: by car across America: a page of simple prose like the setting of a jewel; then a poem as a jewel. Well, we will talk about this. Much love to Carol,

6.8 The second page of Wright's comments on Bly's translation of Neruda's "Compañeros de Viaje": "I felt so happy reading . . . Neruda's poem, gaining for the first time some really clearer and deeper understanding of the man's nobility . . ."

> Were these things dark shadows,
> were they only hidden damp leaves stirred up from the soil?
> What was the wounded substance from which death was pour-
> ing out
> until it touched my arms and legs, controlled my smile,
> and dug a well of pain in the streets?

I went out into life: I grew and was hardened,
I walked through the hideous back alleys
without compassion, singing out on the frontiers
of delirium. The walls filled with faces:
eyes that did not look at the light, twisted waters
lit up by a crime, legacies
of solitary pride, holes
filled with hearts that had been condemned and torn down.
I walked with them: it was only in that chorus
that my voice refound the solitudes
where it was born.

I finally became a man
singing among the flames, accepted
by friends who find their place in the night,
who sang with me in the taverns,
and who gave me more than a single kindness,
something they had defended with their fighting hands,
which was more than a spring,
a fire unknown elsewhere, the natural foliage
of the places slowly falling down at the city's edge.

OCEAN

Whether out of your naked green phantom,
or your immeasurable apple tree, or
your mazurka in the darkness, where
do you come from?
Night
even fresher than the night, salt
mother, bleeding salt, bent mother of water,
planet overtaken by spume and marrow:
enormous kindness with a longitude of stars:
night with a solitary wing in its hand:
storm opposing the sea-going eagle,
blind under the hands of sulfate beyond sounding:
wine-cellar entombed in so much night,

corolla wholly frozen by invasions and noises,
cathedral sunken suddenly into a star.

There is a wounded horse that ran for an age
over your shore, his place is taken by a cold fire,
there is a red fir tree transformed into plumage
and the terrible glassware shattered in your hands,
and the enduring rose attacked on the islands
and the diadem of water and moon that you build.

My homeland, for your earth
all the secret heaven!
All this fruit open to all, this
amazing crown!

I give you this goblet of foam where the sunbeam
is lost like a blind albatross, where the sun climbs
from the south, gazing upon your holy place.

JORGE GUILLÉN (1893–1984)

THE SNOW

The white is upon the green,
And it sings.
The fine snow longs
To grow high.
January is drunk on snow, so green,
So white.
Grown drunk, day and night, on the snow,
The clear snow.
Light snow, smooth flake,
How much warmth massed together!
The snow, snow in the hands
And in the soul.
So pure, the warmth in the whiteness,
So pure, without flame.

The snow, the snow rises
Toward music.
January is drunk on the snow that grows wild.
How much warmth! And it sings.
The snow carries you off—the snow, the snow,
Flying upward, toward music.

THE SHADOWS

Sunshine. Windowshade moving.
Shadows tremble—Who is entering?
. . . They escape. I am: footsteps.
(Oh, with the flickering
Of an eyelid, windowshade
Of loneliness of love!)
I want it transparent.
And I want the shadows, also,
Transparent and happy.
(The shadows, so coldly aloof,
Were dreaming of the palm
Of a hand in a caress!)
My hand, perhaps? But
No, I can't reach. The shadows
Are intangible: dreams.

THE GARDEN WITHIN

   for Emilio

      warm and chiseled clarity
            Gabriel Miró

Flat roofs, turrets, domes
Approximate the desires
Of the streets and public squares
       For their heaven.

       Holiday.
Clouds, clouds of amusement!

Slow, unattached, they
Shift, wander without a goal.

A luminous circle.
A city blurred from within,
May, unhastening toward June
Abandons itself to its own interval.

Into a wholesome disorder:
            Winds itself
Silently. Pleasant noise.

Walled in by the uproar,
Surely no one is far away
From the reality
            Of a miracle.

O sunny isolation,
            Composure of spirit,
Everything keeps its face to the sun,
            Under the wind.

            Purifying hour.
The line of fir trees
            Traces to the very bottom
Its horizon of dark green.

For whom will a blackbird cry?
            The warbling
Surges out of young leaves
            Stirring.

And yet, two ash trees question
            And answer each other.
Even the necks of birds appear foolish,
            Puffed up.

And a plenty of butterflies,
Extending the flutter of their wings,

6.9 An early notebook version of Wright's translation of Guillén's "The Garden Within," which he describes as: "the beautiful garden of safety and happiness, a kind of Eden which we all seek; and then harsh reality breaks in . . . the garden remains 'within'—within us."

Riskily, over the tremulous
Corollas of their reflections.

Between the light and the fragrance
A sweet-toothed insect passes
With bewildered eagerness,
That deepens into rapture.

Even as the daisies
Have a kingdom, off in the distance,
With some yellow bud or other,
Happy at being a solid form.

And a quick water combs out
Glitter on glitter, smiling.
The shadow on the margins
Is scattered like fresh air.

What comely warmth! An environment
        In hiding,
Bench, foliage, penumbra,
        Immense sunlight.

Will so much beauty spill over?
        I want it to spill.
Maybe a slow, useless
        Joy is enough.

        Paradise:
Garden, peace without an owner,
        And some man
In his serene moment.

So much exchange of meaning,
Unresting between the extremes
Of motion, delights me farther
Than many things that I look for.

Broad free space, lawn,
Elm alone in the center,
And my silence, mastered,
        After a struggle!

But . . . another time? Look there,
        Gathered again,
The discordant world, turning
        So alien.

Through the air
With a suspended murmur,
            Float many crossthreads
Of other voices and other presences.

Happiness, the smallest happiness:
Who will uproot you
From this fact of living? Living
Still, and dying so certain!

Here is reality,
Tangled: a raucous confusion.
And the garden? Where is a garden?
Within.

MIGUEL HERNÁNDEZ (1910–1942)

from *El Hombre Acecha*, 1939

THE TRAIN OF THE WOUNDED

Silence that shipwrecks in the silence
of the closed mouths during the night.
It never stops being silent, even when cut across.
It speaks the drowned tongue of the dead.

Open the roads of deep cotton,
muffle the wheels, the clocks,
hold back the voice of the sea, of the pigeon:
stir up the night of dreams.

Silence.

The soaked train of escaping blood,
the frail train of men bleeding to death,
the silent, the painful train, the pale train,
the speechless train of agonies.

Silence.

Train of the deathly pallor that is ascending:
the pallor dresses the heads,
the "ah!", the voice, the heart, the dust,
the heart of those who were badly wounded.

Silence.

They go, spilling legs, arms, eyes,
they go, throwing chunks through the train.
They pass, leaving bitter traces,
a new Milky Way, with their own members for stars.

Silence.

Hoarse train, disheartened, blood-red:
The coal lies in its last agony, the smoke heavily breathes,
and, maternal, the engine sighs,
it moves on, like a long discouragement.

Silence.

The long mother would like to come to a stop
Under a tunnel, and lie down weeping.
There are no way stations for us,
except in the hospital, or else in the breast.

To live a mere bit is enough:
in a single corner of flesh, you can put up a man.
One finger alone, one piece of a wing alone
can lift the whole body into absolute flight.

Silence.

Stop that dying train
that never completes its journey across the night.
Even the dying horse is left without shoes,
and the hooves, and the breath, are buried under the sand.

WAR

All the mothers in the world
hide their wombs, tremble,
and wish they could turn back
into blind virginities,
into that solitary beginning,
the past, with nothing before it.
Virginity is left
pale, frightened.
The sea howls thirst and the earth
howls to be water.
Hatred flames out
and the screaming slams doors.
Voices shake like lances,
voices like bayonets.
Mouths step forward like fists,
fists arrive like hooves.
Breasts like hoarse walls,
legs like sinewy paws.
The heart quickens,
storms, blows up.
It throws sudden black spume
into the eye.
Blood thrashes about in the body,
flings the head off,
and searches for another body, a wound
to leap through, outside.
Blood parades through the world,
caged, baffled.
Flowers wither
devoured by the grass.
A lust for murder possesses
the secret places of the lily.

Every living body longs to be joined
to a piece of cold metal:
to be married and possessed horribly.
To disappear: a vast anxiety,
spreading, rules everything.
A ghostly procession of banners,
a fantastic flag,
a myth of nations: a
grave fiction of frontiers.
Outraged musics,
tough as boots, scar
the face of every hope
and the tender core.
The soul rages, fury.
Tears burst like lightning.
What do I want with light
if I stumble into darkness?
Passions like horns,
songs, trumpets that urge
the living to eat the living,
to tear themselves down stone by stone.
Whinnies. Reverberations. Thunder.
Slaverings. Kisses. Wheels.
Spurs. Crazy swords
tear open a huge wound.
Then silence, mute
as cotton, white as bandages,
scarlet as surgery,
mutilated as sadness.
Silence. And laurel
in a corner among bones.
And a hysterical drum,
a tense womb, beats
behind the innumerable
dead man who never gets past.

Often at public readings Wright would recite from memory his own translation of the Spanish poet Pedro Salinas's gorgeous love poem "Not in Marble Palaces." It is easy to see why Wright loved this poem, and included it in his *Collected Poems* (1971). It has so much of what he aspires to in his own work—restraint, clarity, tenderness, and candor—in a poem that shows love outside of time or place, outside the past or future, independent of the world's history and materialism:

Not in marble palaces,
not in months, no, not in ciphers,
never touching ground:
in weightless, fragile worlds
we have lived together.
Time was beaten out,
but hardly by minutes:
one minute was a hundred years,
one life, one love.
Roofs sheltered us,
less than roofs, clouds;
less than clouds, heavens;
even less, air, nothing.
Crossing oceans
formed out of twenty tears,
ten yours and ten mine,
we arrived at the golden
beads of a necklace,
clear islands, deserted,
without flowers, without bodies;
a harbor so tiny,
made of glass, for a love
that in itself was enough
for the largest longing,
and we asked neither ships
nor time for help.
Opening
enormous tunnels

in grains of sand,
we discovered the mines
of flames and chance.
And everything
hanging from that thread
that held up . . . what?
That's why our life
doesn't appear to be lived:
slippery, evasive,
it left behind neither wakes
nor footprints. If you want
to remember it, don't look
where you always look for traces
and recollections.

Then Wright spoke the last lines in slightly hushed tones:

Don't look at your soul,
your shadows or your lips.
Look carefully into the palm
of your hand, it's empty.

When he'd finished, he would pause for a moment, extend his right
arm, open his hand, and display his empty palm.

7. Georg Trakl's "Grodek" Translated by James Wright and Robert Bly: A Portfolio

JEFFREY KATZ

"You should see us working together on something. We get up in the morning and won't even look at each other. We pace back and forth."[1]

James Wright on his collaboration with Robert Bly

James Wright had worked on translating Georg Trakl poems as early as 1952 while on a Fulbright scholarship in Vienna, and then in 1954 he took up Trakl again with careful attention in the graduate program he attended at the University of Washington (see chapter 2). In 1957 he published his own first book, *The Green Wall*, began publishing widely in journals, and appeared, along with Robert Bly, in the conservative anthology *New Poets of England and America*, edited by Donald Hall, Robert Pack, and Louis Simpson. Bly described his reaction to that anthology this way: "I knew there was something wrong with the poetry of the men and women my age, because it wasn't flowing somehow, or it didn't penetrate downwards. I didn't feel touched by it. I didn't feel it with my soul."[2]

In 1958, the first issue of Bly's journal *The Fifties* came out. He sent copies to all of the recent anthology's contributors, including James Wright. Wright returned a long letter almost immediately, describing what he understood Bly to be saying, relating that to the reading Wright had been doing of Trakl, and calling this the "new imagination."[3] Bly replied with a long letter of his own: "I am overjoyed that you feel the phrase 'new imagination' conveys something. We must have some sort of phrase to describe these dark waters of Neruda, Lorca, Trakl and the poems made of a new substance I've never seen before."[4] In remembering this time in the 1970s, Bly recounted: "[Wright] said *The Fifties* gave him some hope there might be a way out—he asked if he could come see me. He did and we became friends right away. It turned out that Trakl was crucial—a wholly new road for him . . . Jim and I became friends partly because we both felt something deep and strong in Trakl."[5]

Along with their individual work on Trakl and Neruda, throughout the late 1950s and early 1960s Wright and Bly were also working on their own poems in this emerging new style, which would become their books *Silence in the Snowy Fields* (1962) and *The Branch Will Not Break* (1963). Bly wrote of the time: "Well, those years were a moment of genuine longing for a fresh and subtle poetry; there was so much joy at finding great Spanish and German poets."[6]

In the meantime, they collaborated very closely, trading versions of Trakl poems back and forth and trying out individual lines and phrases, a process they would subsequently use many times over the years with Vallejo, Neruda, Lorca, and others. In the fall of 1958, they wrote long letters back and forth and met at the Bly farm in Minnesota to work over the Trakl translations. The letters excerpted and the notebook pages reproduced here afford readers a unique opportunity to watch the collaboration of these two great friends at close range.

Thanks to the survival of a spiral notebook Wright kept at the time, readers are now able to take a close look at the trials, errors, extravagances, and triumphs of his efforts during September 1958 to make an English version of Georg Trakl's last poem, "Grodek." In September of 1914, Trakl had returned to active military service as a lieutenant attached to the Medical Corps of the Austrian army in Galicia. "Grodek" and "Klage" (Lament) were the only poems he would write in the field.

Although not all of Wright's notebook pages are dated, what appears to be his earliest is dated September 5, 1958, and the one marked "Done; Send to Bly" is marked September 29, 1958. A year later, Wright is still working at "Grodek" and sends a letter to the Blys along with four Trakl translations, including his latest version of "Grodek," changed slightly:

Sept. 29, 1959

Dear Carol and Bob,

Here are the results of the latest foray into modern life. I can fill a note with comments, but that's just my old way of beating around the bush. It should be enough to say, for the moment, that these four enclosed translations follow your comments pretty closely. However, you'll notice that I've made a few changes in GRODEK from what the three of us had achieved. Your note "imagine the situation of the poem, which is not stated, before you translate" has me reading Trakl endlessly, brooding about him, speaking these short poems aloud, trying to act out the various identities that appear in them as in a kind of shadow play; and I think that I understand GRODEK now—if not all the way down into its most profound recesses, then at least down far enough to reveal some buried treasures. You will wonder about the first three lines: the point is to introduce "deadly weapons" casually (your own observation on understatement) in the midst of the pastoral images, and I think this is best done in our language by simply and without strain (your notes on this problem were really a revelation) listing the four images: the autumn forests, the golden meadows, the blue lakes—I see something like a landscape by Renoir, rich in color but covered by deliberate haze—and then, almost as an afterthought (as though the poet were saying, "And, oh yes, I forgot to mention something—), the flat statement that this pastoral landscape is now possessed by deadly weapons, like worms in beautiful yellow apples. It is starting to become clear that Trakl in many poems (like IN THE EAST, above), deliberately places pastoral and harsh urban (or war) imagery side by side, underplays both, and lets a kind of explosion flare up and join them together . . .[7]

In all, four versions of Wright's "Grodek" translation and two of
Bly's are included here (see figures 7.1–7.7), representing the likely
chronological order, along with the German text and a plain prose
translation of the German by Leonard Wilson Forster from *The Pen-*
guin Book of German Verse (1959), and, finally, "Grodek" as published
in *Twenty Poems of Georg Trakl* (1961) and reprinted in Bly's *The Winged*
Energy of Delight: Selected Translations (2004).

GRODEK

Am Abend tönen die herbstlichen Wälder
Von tödlichen Waffen, die goldnen Ebenen
Und blauen Seen, darüber die Sonne
Düstrer hinrollt; umfängt die Nacht
Sterbende Krieger, die wilde Klage
Ihrer zerbrochenen Münder.
Doch stille sammelt im Weidengrund
Rotes Gewölk, darin ein zürnender Gott wohnt
Das vergoßne Blut sich, mondne Kühle;
Alle Straßen münden in schwarze Verwesung.
Unter goldenem Gezweig der Nacht und Sternen
Es schwankt der Schwester Schatten durch den schweigenden
    Hain,
Zu grüßen die Geister der Helden, die blutenden Häupter;
Und leise tönen im Rohr die dunkeln Flöten des Herbstes.
O stolzere Trauer! ihr ehernen Altäre
Die heiße Flamme des Geistes nährt heute ein gewaltiger
    Schmerz,
Die ungeborenen Enkel.[8]

GRODEK

Leonard Wilson Forster, translator

In the evening the autumnal forests resound with the noise
of deadly weapons, the golden plains and the blue lakes over
which the sinister sun rolls onward; night embraces dying war-
riors, the wild lament of their shattered mouths. But silently,

Sept. 5, 1958:

Grodek

In the autumnal gloaming the forests resound
With howitzers... ~~and~~ meadows of golden line
And lakes of azure, and above them the sun
Falling ~~away~~ in dark flight; the night receives the
Recruits into her ~~b~~ arms, the animal mourning
Of their broken mouths.

All roads lead to the same ~~black dead~~ corruption
Under the ~~golden~~ night's golden branch; under
the stars.
The sister's shadow falters through the
To welcome the ghosts of our boys, bleeding heads;
And lightly the dark flutes of the year's fall resound
in the reeds.

You men of distinction! You altars molded of bronze,
What makes the soul's fire leap up is an intense suffering,
The children yet unborn.

7.1 The earliest version of Wright's translation of Trakl's "Grodek," a rough sketch of most of the poem's seventeen lines, dated September 5, 1958.

in the willow-grown hollow there gathers a red cloud in which a wrathful god lives—the shed blood, moonlike coolness; all roads end in black decay. Beneath the golden branches of night and stars my sister's shadow wavers through the silent wood to greet the spirits of the heroes, the bleeding heads; and in the reeds the dark flutes of autumn softly sound. O prouder morning! you brazen altars, today the hot flame of the spirit is fed by a tremendous pain: the unborn grandchildren.[9]

The earliest version of Wright's translation (see figure 7.1) is a rough sketch, dated September 5, 1958, of most of the poem's seventeen lines, which display many of the virtues and defects of early drafts of his own poems. He uses the overelaborate "gloaming" for Trakl's simple "Am Abend" ("In the evening"); the unnecessarily indirect "meadows of golden hue" and "lakes of azure" rather than Trakl's straightforward golden plains and blue lakes. Early on, Wright was inserting his own sensibilities over Trakl's. In fact, Bly counsels him in a letter in October to lower his voice: "The odd thing is that the lower your voice becomes, the more powerful your words are, and the more ominous and effective the poem becomes."[10]

Wright's experimental use of "howitzers" in line 2 wouldn't survive beyond the earliest versions, but it is a fascinating trial for Trakl's "tödlichen Waffen," which others translate as "deadly weapons," "weapons of death," or "lethal weapons." "Howitzers" refers to a particularly deadly weapon used in Europe since the fifteenth century and steadily "improved" until Krupp was hurrying them into production in time for World War I. The origin of the word is Czech by way of Middle High German: "Haufen" meaning "crowd," that is, a weapon made to fire on a crowd—a mass of soldiers, a charging cavalry, a teeming trench. And "howitzers" would surface again in Wright's poem "Echo for the Promise of Georg Trakl's Life," first published in *The New Yorker* in 1970. In it Wright compares the generative silence of Trakl's voice to the stuttering guns that make no true sound: "Quiet voice, / In the midst of those blazing / Howitzers in blossom." The specificity of "howitzers," though, is an odd choice given the abstractness of Trakl's poem, the strange lack of human presence in a war poem written by a combatant in a terrible battle. Trakl's way throughout the poem is exactly the opposite of particulars like "howitzers." His choices are aimed at mythologizing or universalizing the details of the battle in order to make them timeless.

In line 5, Wright again chooses the more particular, less literary "recruits" for "Sterbende Krieger" ("dying warriors"), preferring the connotation of young, recently enlisted, inexperienced soldiers. Trakl's original choice reflects the mythic perspective of his treatment of the battle. When he wanted to say "dying soldiers," as in a poem like his "Im Osten" (In the East), he writes "sterbende Soldat." He uses the figure of "warriors" ("Krieger") here and "heroes" ("Helden") later in the poem, and for the same reasons uses the more general "deadly weapons" ("tödlichen Waffen") in line 2.

Wright allows "the cries of their broken mouths" to stand in for "dying." In this first version, we see him thinking through the wild cries of these dying boys and joins these boys to the maternal image of the night in line 4 "receiv[ing] them in her arms" like infants. For Trakl's "umfängt," or "embrace," he first uses "receives" and later "lifts" and then, weirdly, "captures," before finally deciding on "lifts dying / recruits in its arms," unfortunately abandoning the explicit maternal expression.

In his next attempt (figure 7.2) Wright tries out "weapons of murder" for "todlichen Waffen" and relates the sound of the weapons in line 1's "blares out" with line 14's "sound[ing] out" of the dark flutes. He also keeps the word order of Trakl's German in this version, although the phrasing drifts around in his next drafts.

There seems to be no compelling reason in terms of either semantic or sonic effect for Wright to switch the position of the landscape description, "golden meadows and blue lakes," as he does (see figures 7.3 and 7.4), with the source of the reverberation in the woods, "deadly weapons." But see Wright's justifications in the September 29, 1959 letter on page 185. In response, Bly writes in an October 9 letter: "I doubt if one can alter the order of the opening sentences of Grodek so drastically as to put the golden meadows & blue lakes before the deadly weapons, rather than after—they look different also, as if seen through colored glasses, after the mind has taken in the concept "tödlichen Waffen." And yet it might be asserted that the deafening presence of those heavy guns and the shells they fire will change the landscape forever, and that the lake and meadows are only blue and golden in the imagination now. This emphasis on the foreclosure of the future returns in the final three lines, with the moving invocation of the unborn future generations.

Opportunities are missed in these early drafts, as well as in some of the later ones, to include Trakl's emphasis on sounds. ("Tönen" is a word he uses often in his poems.) He moves from the deep sounds

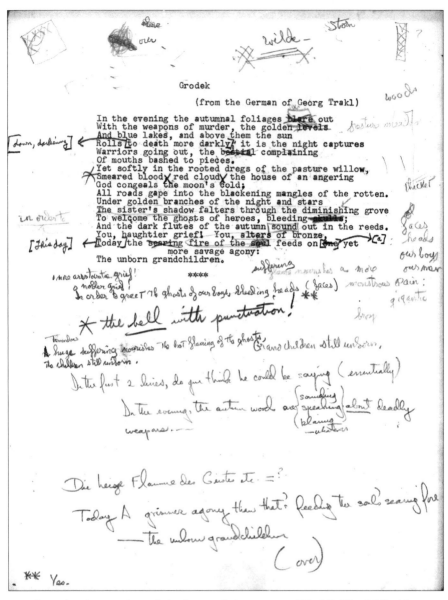

7.2 An undated typescript early in the translation process of Trakl's "Grodek," with notes by both Wright and Bly, and with Wright's urgent scrawl: "* to hell with punctuation!"

of artillery, to the cries of the recruits under fire, to the silent copse, to the whisper of the reeds in the wind. The forest "blares out" in line 1, which seems a better choice than "sounds" or "resounds" for the hideous rumble of heavy guns, even though "sounds" is closer to the German.

Bly complains of Wright's final choice of "trembles" for this sound, arguing that "'tremble' is a too thin reverberation, I think—the poem has huge reverberations, like an organ."[11] This is an acute observation about the kind of deep, bone-shaking sound made by heavy artillery, but is not demonstrated in the published version of the translation. The "bestial complaining" in line 5, not clearly called for in the German, is greatly improved by the simpler "wild cries" in draft 3, retained by Wright until his "final" draft, which shows that he also tried out "bleating" and (fortunately) rejected it.

In October, Bly tells Wright that "'Allen Strassen munden in schwarze Verwesung' [all roads lead to black decay] in line 10 still isn't caught by me or you. [A] German woman who was here the other day said it suggests that all flesh decays . . . we still haven't got 'tödlichen Waffen'—as I understand it, this is a phrase some half-crazed widow might scream on a battlefield—but no widow would scream 'deadly weapons' nor 'arms that wound to death!' Looked at this way, I don't know which phrase is the more ridiculous."

Yet in keeping with Trakl's mythologizing approach, perhaps "weapons of death" is appropriate. The phrase is general enough, but the *x of y* construction of this expression interestingly suggests both "weapons made of death" and "weapons belonging to death." In the version published in *Twenty Poems of Georg Trakl* (1961) and later reprinted in Bly's *The Winged Energy of Delight: Selected Translations* (2004), Bly settles for the rather clunky "All the roads spread out into the black mold," along with "weapons of death." This is an improvement of "weapons that wound to death" for sure, but using the "crazed widow" test, would she be likely to shout "weapons of death," either? Clearly, Trakl doesn't intend a realistic description of the battlefield at Grodek. Instead, following his work's expressionist/imagistic aesthetic, he creates a symbolic landscape emphasizing the universal

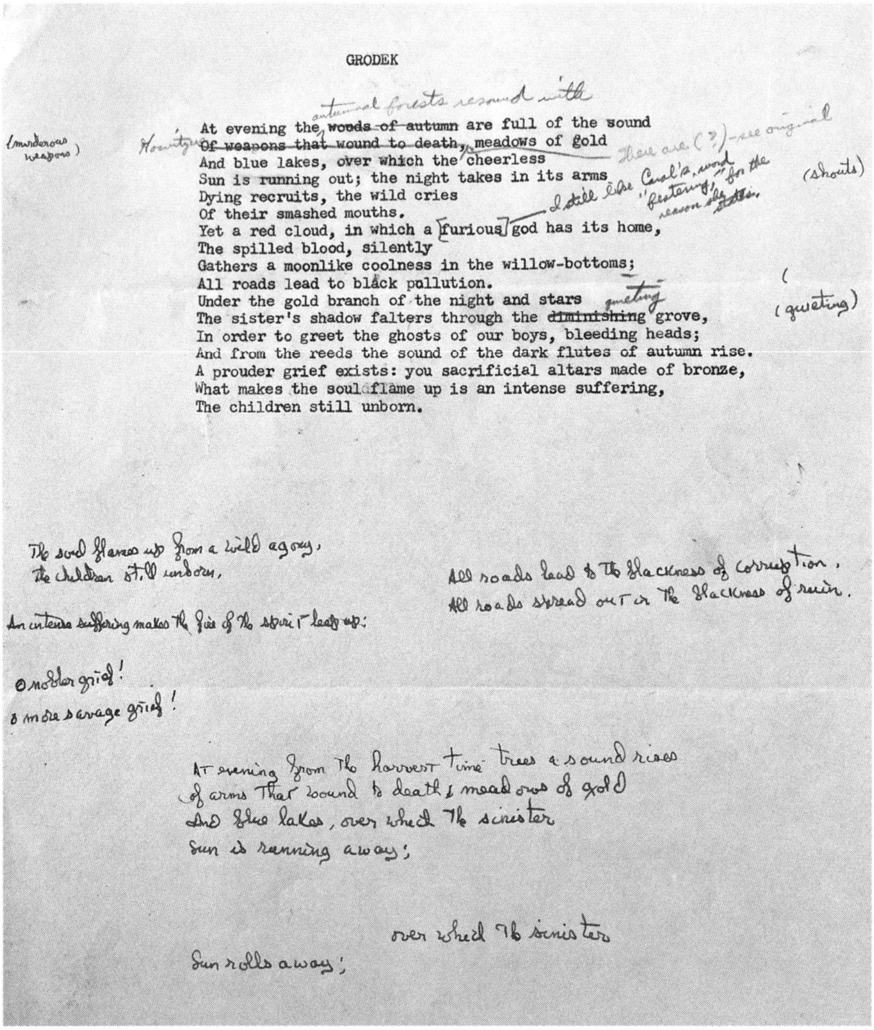

GRODEK

At evening the woods of autumn are full of the sound
Of weapons that wound to death, meadows of gold
And blue lakes, over which the cheerless
Sun is running out; the night takes in its arms
Dying recruits, the wild cries
Of their smashed mouths.
Yet a red cloud, in which a furious god has its home,
The spilled blood, silently
Gathers a moonlike coolness in the willow-bottoms;
All roads lead to black pollution.
Under the gold branch of the night and stars
The sister's shadow falters through the diminishing grove,
In order to greet the ghosts of our boys, bleeding heads;
And from the reeds the sound of the dark flutes of autumn rise.
A prouder grief exists: you sacrificial altars made of bronze,
What makes the soul flame up is an intense suffering,
The children still unborn.

[Handwritten marginal notes, partly legible:]

(murderous weapons) — *autumnal forests resound with* — *There are (?) — see original* — *(shouts)* — *I still like Carol's word "festering" for the reason ...* — *(quieting)*

[Handwritten notes below:]

The soul flames up from a wild agony,
the children still unborn.

An intense suffering makes the fire of the spirit leap up:

O nobler grief!
O more savage grief!

At evening from the harvest time trees a sound rises
of arms that wound to death, meadows of gold
And blue lakes, over which the sinister
Sun is running away;

over which the sinister
Sun rolls away;

All roads lead to the blackness of corruption,
All roads spread out in the blackness of ruin.

7.3 An early, undated typescript of Bly's effort at the "Grodek" translation, with notes by both Bly and Wright.

over the particular, and the oracular ("O haughtier grief, you bronze altars") over the impressionistic.

At the same time, Bly was trying out his own ideas for the translation, with handwritten suggestions by Wright (see figure 7.3).[12]

Bly at this stage accepts several of Wright's innovations: "dying recruits" for "sterbende Krieger," and "willows-bottoms" for "Weidengrund." Trakl's "schwarze Verwesung" undergoes several changes

Trakl: Grodek (_Dichtungen_, p. 197)

In the evening the autumnal forests blare out
With the weapons of murder, the golden levels
And blue lakes, and above them the sun
Rolls downward more darkly; it is the night captures
~~Dying~~ ~~the~~
Perishing ~~the~~ warriors; the bestial complaining
Of mouths crushed to ~~pieces.~~
Yet softly in the dregs of the willows
Red cloud, the ~~sentence~~ of an angering ~~god,~~
                house
The spilled blood congeals the moon's cold;
Every road gapes into black ~~corruption~~ putrefaction.
Under golden branches of the night and stars
The sister's shadow ~~staggers~~ through the diminishing grove
              falters
To welcome the ghosts of heroes, the bleeding skulls.
And the dark ~~flutes of the autumnal~~ of autumn ~~sound out~~
in the reeds.
You, ~~statelier~~ grief! You ne altars of bronze,
~~a mighty~~
       daughter
[Today a more powerful agony feeds the ~~softly~~]
Today the seeing fire of the soul feeds an a more powerful agony
The unborn grandchildren.
                               yet

7.4   On an undated notebook page, Wright renders line 10 of "Grodek" as "Every road gapes into black corruption," then crosses out the last word and inserts "putrefaction."

until they finally land on the vague "black mold" in the printed version. Trakl uses "Verwesung" to mean "decay" seven times in his _Die Dichtungen_ and uses "Fäulnis" three times specifically to indicate "rot." Bly suggests "black pollution" early on and Wright tries out "blackened corruption" (see figure 7.1), "mangles of the rotten" (figure 7.2), and "putrefaction" (figure 7.3), before he settles on "black decay" (figure 7.4 and 7.5).

Trakl's most syntactically intricate lines, 7–9, are completely omitted from Wright's first draft (figure 7.1). Their literal translation might be:

7.5 Another of Wright's undated notebook pages, including four different attempts at translating the thorny line 10 of "Grodek."

But silently collects in the willow-ground
red clouds in which an angry god dwells
the spilled blood, moon coolness.

The first version of Wright's to include these lines has:

Yet softly in the rooted dregs of the pasture willow,
Smeared blood[,] red cloud[,] the house of an angering
God congeals the moon's cold (figure 7.2)

Below this draft, Wright scrawls "*the hell with punctuation!*"
His next version has:

Yet softly in the dregs of the willows
Red cloud, the house of an angering god,
The spilled blood congeals the moon's cold (figure 7.3)

Then in a new version (figure 7.5) he works hard at a new word order, new vocabulary, and new semantic solutions, overflowing into the margins of his page:

Yet a red cloud, where a <u>festering</u> god has its home

He tries out several alternatives for line 7:

the moon cools the brow of the feverish god
where feverish with anger a god/a god feverish with anger has
    his home
the god feverish ("*That's it!,*" he writes)

and in line 8 he continues:

The spilled blood, silently
Gathers ~~a moonlike~~ coolness of the moon in the willow bottoms

then again comments in the margin: "*i.e. the moon has now risen to cool the red god*" . . .
The completed version (figure 7.5) reads:

Yet a red cloud, where the feverish god has its home
The spilled blood, silently,
Gathers coolness of the moon in the willow bottoms (figure 7.6)

The version marked "Done Sept. 29, 1958; send to Bly" offers these "final," though still somewhat tentative, lines 7–9:

Georg Trakl's "Grodek": A Portfolio   195

7.6 Wright's notebook version marked "Done Sept. 29, 58; send to Bly." Note the still somewhat tentative proposals for lines 5 and 10.

Yet a red cloud, where a god feverish with anger lodges,
The spilled blood, silently
Gathers coolness of the moon in the willow bottoms (figure 7.6)

A handwritten draft, undated but probably from late September 1958, shows Bly struggling with these same lines.13 (See figure 7.7.)

In his brief introduction to *Twenty Poems of Georg Trakl*, "The Silence of Georg Trakl," Bly writes that Trakl's poems have "a magnificent silence in them . . . for the most part he allows the images to speak for him." Bly describes this silence as "the silence of things that could speak, but choose not to."14 As an example of the voices of things that Trakl permits to speak, Bly cites the "blood that had

A red cloud, in which a furious god has its home,
The spilled blood, a moonlike coolness
Silently gathers in the willow bottoms;
All roads end in rottenness turning black.

Yet a red cloud, in which a furious god has his home,
silently gathers together the scattered blood, cold as the moon.

A red cloud, the blood that is spilled, in which a furious
god has his home, silently gathers in the willow bottoms,
cold as the moon.

Yet red clouds, in which a furious god, the spilled
blood itself, has its home, silently gathers a moonlike
coolness in the willow bottoms.

Grodek

At evening, from the harvest-time trees a sound rises
of arms that wound to death, meadows of gold
And blue lakes, over which the sinister
Sun rolls away; the night takes in its arms
Dying recruits, the wild shouts
of their smashed mouths.
Yet in red cloud, in which a furious god has his home,
The spilled blood, silently
Gathers a moonlike coolness in the willow bottoms;

Under the gold branch of the night and stars
The sisters shadow falters through the quieting grove,
In order to greet the ghosts of our boys, bleeding heads;
And from the reeds the sounds of the dark flutes of autumn rise.
O nobler grief! you altars made of bronze,

The soul flames up from a wild agony,
The children still unborn.
The soul flames up from a wild agony,
The children still unborn.

[marginal notes:]
of deathlike weapons,
pouring down
pastures
night raises
All roads drop off into black soakage.
earth
rottenness
into rottenblack.
A nobler grief offers:
the soul flames up from an intense suffering:
O more savage grief

run from the wounds of that day" on the battlefield at Grodek. The red cloud at the dead center of the poem with its nearly impenetrable syntax forces on us an unimaginable scene that nevertheless must be imagined. Bly make no less than five different attempts at these crucial lines.

In the version finally printed in *Twenty Poems of Georg Trakl* three years later, lines 7–9 read:

> Yet a red cloud, in which a furious god,
> The spilled blood itself, has its home, silently
> Gathers, a moonlike coolness in the willow bottoms;

The translations in *Twenty Poems* were not attributed individually to either Wright or Bly, and this final version seems to bear the mark of both poets. In fact, in a letter to Wright dated May 9, 1959, Bly identifies both poets as translators of "Grodek." The published version of lines 7–9 attempts to regularize Trakl's syntax a bit more than before, lines are rearranged, and at least one newly suggestive idea is added. In line 8, the god becomes "the spilled blood itself."

In some ways, the impenetrability of these lines helps create their evocation of the hallucinatory terror of battle. Trakl's language may be difficult, but is it impossible to read the scene—even if not entirely realistically? Could it be said that a low-lying wetland at the base of the trees has been created by all the spilled blood of the battle of Grodek collecting there? Could it be understood that like the formation of fog in the cool early morning, a red cloud, a kind of bloody vapor, develops over this wetland, in which a furious god, perhaps a timelessly insatiable one, moves? Anywhere one steps, he steps through blackening corpses. So, the scene has a supernatural aspect as well. Gods move among men, even as they did at Troy. And this connection to the timeless memory is doubtless what Robert Bly was thinking of.

Lines 12–14 turn away from the nightmarish battleground to a scene of consecration, or reconciliation of sorts, as a "sister," a nurse, or "sister of mercy" (or, as others suggest, a Valkyrie) appears to greet the recruits now transformed into the spirits of heroes bearing their still-fresh wounds. The translating poets don't completely deliver on the challenge of Trakl's marvelously sibilant line 14: "es Schwankt der Schwester Schatten durch den schweigenden Hain." In his first two drafts (figure 7.1 and 7.2) Wright chose the evocative "falters" for Trakl's "Schwankt," as if she were hesitant, as if she were picking her way through the trees. He then tried "staggers" in the third version (figure 7.3), a better choice to maintain the alliteration, but not a good one semantically, and he crossed it out and reinserted "falters," which he leaves in the remainder of his versions. Bly retains "falters," too. The German suggests that "sway" might have conveyed a similar feeling and retained the sibilance.

Lines 12–14 elaborate on the poem's soundscape. The echo of the heavy guns in the wood in line 2 and the soldiers' "wild cries" in line 5 become once more the "schweigenden Hain," the silent grove of line 12, a grove "that grows silent," or "that grows still" as Wright has it. (See figures 7.4 and 7.5.) But Bly retains the awkward "diminishing grove" in the published translation. The soundscape is then further elaborated by the lovely "leise tönen," conveying the soft sounds of those reeds, "the dark flutes of autumn" in line 14.

With line 15, in the vocative "O stolzere Trauer!," the speaker breaks the frame of the poem, turning to face grief itself, perhaps as a call to a grieving humanity, but characterizing grief as "prouder." Wright, in his earliest draft, made another intriguing choice for translating this phrase that could only have been based on his reading of the poem: "You men of distinction!" "Men of distinction" is not faithful enough to the German to remain in any other Wright drafts, or in the final translation, but it remains in the memory. He tried out "haughtier" (figure 7.3), then settled on "prouder" (figure 7.4 and 7.5), which is retained for the published version. In any case, "stolzere Trauer" suggests the demonstration of grief as part of the usual system of sacrifices, such as might be on display with lofty speeches given by generals and politicians. Yet there seems another or additional choice. Could "prouder grief" refer to the poem itself (or does the speaker address himself?), as if to say: "I am implicated in both the grief and the fury. I offer the poem, but is it enough?" This is a question James Wright struggled with throughout his life.

In the next lines the speaker calls out to the "brazen altars," another mark of the mythical, and invokes a more intense grief even than the grief over these dead heroes, a sacrificial flame that engulfs the soul by calling to mind "the grandsons never born," a pain that overwhelms even today's pain. Wright renders these lines in his final version (figure 7.5): "The soul's flame leaps up to an intense suffering, / To children still unborn." The "furious god" of line 8 has gotten what he wanted. Here, today ("heute"), the timeless warriors and heroes, the deadly weapons and receiving night and holy fire intersect with the present moment and burn so hotly that it deforms time itself, foreclosing on the future.

As he was boarding the train to Innsbruck to join Austrian troops at the front in August 1914, Trakl scribbled this aphorism on a piece of paper and handed it to his friend and benefactor, Ludwig von Ficker. By October, Trakl was dead.

Feeling in moments of deathlike being: all people are worthy of love. Awakening you feel the bitterness of the world; in it is all your unresolved debt; your poem an imperfect atonement.[15]

From the very start of his career, James Wright's poems were about loss and loneliness and the redemptive power of love, about the value of persons rendered invisible or marginal by the world's bitterness. He was also candid about the ways in which he was implicated, like Trakl, in both the unresolved debt and his poetry's attempt at atonement. Again and again he used his work with translations to access his own tenderness and reverence for a humanism that might transform the bitterness of the world.

Here is the translation of "Grodek" as published in *Twenty Poems of Georg Trakl*, the first volume in *The Fifties/Sixties Translation Series* (1961).

GRODEK

At evening the woods of autumn are full of the sound
Of the weapons of death, golden fields
And blue lakes, over which the darkening sun

Rolls down; night gathers in
Dying recruits, the animal cries
Of their burst mouths.
Yet a red cloud, in which a furious god,
The spilled blood itself, has its home, silently
Gathers, a moonlike coolness in the willow bottoms;
All the roads spread out into the black mold.
Under the gold branches of the night and stars
The sister's shadow falters through the diminishing grove,
To greet the ghosts of the heroes, bleeding heads;
And from the reeds the sound of the dark flutes of autumn rises.
O prouder grief! you bronze altars,
The hot flame of the spirit is fed today by a more monstrous
    pain,
The unborn grandchildren.[16]

Afterword

JEFFREY KATZ

James Wright was a lover of language wherever he found it, a lover of voices and voicings—of pitch and duration, of echo and chiming, of urgency, humor, and tenderness. He had a prodigious memory, and these voicings became, crucially, features of his own voice, whether he was reciting long passages from Dickens's *Great Expectations* or Whitman, Heine, or Jiménez. Translation represented an opportunity to hear differently, to provoke his everyday facility. As Lorca says, ". . . One must break it all up; the dogmas must clean themselves up and the patterns take on new excitement . . ."[1] Ultimately, Wright sought through the work of translation to return more fully to his own language—the one he was always learning to speak. And as we've seen, the translations that he knew as well as his own voice—those of Rilke, Heine, Vallejo, and Catullus—frequently found their way as versions, adaptations, imitations, and echoes in his own verse.

Wright took up these voices, as homage and touchstone, from *The Green Wall* (1957) until *To a Blossoming Pear Tree* (1977), in a dozen different ways. He used as epigraphs for his books and for individual poems quotations from Goethe, Storm, Rilke, Sappho, and Catullus; in his poems, he addressed forebears such as Horace, Neruda, Trakl, Hernandez, and Leopardi; and he wrote imitations and adaptations of Rilke, Heine, Goethe, Horace, Plato, and Anacreon.

So Much Secret Labor traces the Latin, German, and Spanish poems and poets to which James Wright would ever return. Their lovely and sustaining music drifts through his letters, his notebooks, and all of his published work. His first translations included Catullus's Carmina 3, "Ode to Lesbia's Pet Sparrow," enclosed with a letter to his high school English teacher Elizabeth Willerton Esterly in 1947. Thirty years later lines from that poem reappear in Latin but revised for his poem "One Last Look at the Adige: Verona in the Rain":

> The unrighteous heathen,
> Valerio Catullo,
> Was born in Verona,
> And you held him in the curve of your arm.
> He couldn't stand it.
> He left home and went straight
> To hell in Rome.
> *Io factum male io miselle*
> *Adige*, the lights
> Have gone out on the stone bridge,
> Where I stand alone,
> A dark city on one shore,
> And, on the other,
> A dark forest.

From Italy, just months before his death in 1980, the poet wrote to a former school friend from Martins Ferry, Ohio:

> At the moment, this early evening, I'm sitting by the window of an old hotel, looking over Lake Garda. The building is located about halfway out the long, green peninsula called Sirmione. I wonder if you remember a little poem printed toward the back of Miss Sheriff's old beginner's text in Latin. It begins "*Paene insularum, Sirmio, insularumque ocelle* . . ." (Almost an island, Sirmio, eye of islands.) The lines are by the ancient Roman Catullus.[2]

In the end, the work here is not the solution to a mystery, not the hunting out of clues and sources (although much hunting was carried out), but the careful illumination of the steady work with translations that the poet himself called "so much secret labor." It is a story of friendship, of something like rescue, of the opening up to new form and the plain, daily, hard work of moving line by line through poems.

Notes

Abbreviations

The following abbreviations are used for frequently cited works:

AWP   Anne Wright and Saundra Rose Maley, eds., with Jonathan Blunk, *A Wild Perfection: The Selected Letters of James Wright* (New York: Farrar, Straus and Giroux, 2005).

CP   James Wright, *Collected Prose*, ed. Anne Wright (Ann Arbor: University of Michigan Press, 1982).

PCW   Dave Smith, ed., *The Pure Clear Word: Essays on the Poetry of James Wright* (Urbana: University of Illinois Press, 1982).

Preface: James Wright and Translations

1. James Wright to Robert Bly, July 22, 1958, in *AWP*, 111.
2. JW to Robert Bly, July 22, 1958, in *AWP*, 111.

Introduction: James Wright and the Sound of the Human Voice

1. Unpublished draft, James Wright papers, Upper Midwest Literary Archives, University of Minnesota Libraries, Minneapolis, Minnesota (hereafter cited as UMLA).
2. JW, letter to "A Young Writer," February 19, 1959, UMLA (hereafter cited as JW).
3. JW, letter to "A Young Writer," April 8, 1959, UMLA.
4. JW, letter to "A Young Writer," April 22, 1959, UMLA.
5. JW, letter to "A Young Writer," February 22, 1959, UMLA.
6. JW, *CP*, 182–83.
7. JW, "A Note on Trakl," *CP*, 84.
8. JW, "Meditations on René Char," *CP*, 68.

James Wright Among Other Voices: A Chronology

1. JW, "Childhood Sketch," *CP*, 331.

Chapter 1: First Translations

1. JW, letter to James L. McCreight, Spring 1946, *AWP*, 5.
2. JW, letter to Elizabeth Willerton, January 6, 1947, *AWP*, 14.
3. JW, letter to Susan Lamb, September 3, 1946, *AWP*, 10–11.
4. JW, letter to Dr. Thomas Hodge, June 8, 1979, *AWP*, 536–37.
5. JW, letter to James L. McCreight, Spring 1946, *AWP*, 6.

Chapter 2: A Solitary Apprenticeship: The German Poets

1. Steve Orlen, "The Green Wall," *Ironwood* 10 (1977): 7.
2. Orlen, 5.
3. JW, "A Complaint for George Doty in the Death House," *The Paris Review* 9 (Summer 1955): 126–7.
4. E. L. Doctorow, "James Wright at Kenyon," in "A Special Feature on James Wright," *Gettysburg Review* 3, no. 1 (Winter 1990): 11–22.
5. From a letter of recommendation JW prepared for Hanfman dated September 29, 1971. A copy of this letter was sent to Saundra Maley by Dara Hanfman, Hanfman's widow.
6. Edwin Spievack interviewed by Saundra Maley on November 11, 1989.
7. JW, unpublished typescript with marginal notes, James Wright papers, Upper Midwest Literary Archives, University of Minnesota Libraries, Minneapolis, Minnesota (hereafter cited as UMLA).
8. JW, letter to Jack Furniss, June 28, 1949. Provided to Saundra Maley by Jack Furniss, December 6, 1989.
9. JW, letter to Jack Furniss, July 28, 1949.
10. JW, "Vision and Elegy (R. M. Rilke d.1926)," *Hika* 15 (Fall 1950): 24–28, digital.kenyon.edu/hika/87, accessed December 12, 2023.
11. JW, unpublished draft, UMLA.
12. JW, unpublished draft, UMLA.
13. JW, unpublished draft, UMLA.
14. JW, letter to Jack Furniss, July 18, 1950.
15. JW, "Kleider machen Lause ein Liederkranz (Clothes Make the Man: A Song Cycle): Some Imitations of Heinrich Heine's German," *Hika* 17 (Winter 1951): 14, digital.kenyon.edu/hika/73, accessed December 12, 2023.
16. JW, in *1954 Student Workbook*, unpaginated, Theodore Roethke Collection, Special Collections, University of Washington Libraries.
17. Heinrich Heine, *Heine: Selected Verse*, trans. Peter Branscombe (Harmondsworth and New York: Penguin, 1986), 24.
18. JW, unpublished manuscript, UMLA.
19. JW, "To a Visitor from My Hometown," *Assay* 14 (Winter/Spring): 8.
20. Walther von der Vogelweide, "Alas! Where Have All the Years Gone?,"

trans. unknown, mypoeticside.com/show-classic-poem-32210, accessed November, 2022.

21. Reprinted in *PCW*, 6.

22. JW, letter to E. L. Doctorow, March 13, 1964, *AWP*, 290.

23. JW, "Elegiac Verses for Theodor Storm," *Hika* 16 (Summer 1951): 10, digital.kenyon.edu/hika/73, accessed December 12, 2023.

24. JW, "Theodor Storm: Foreword," *CP*, 79.

25. JW, "Translator's Note on Herman Hesse, *CP*, 88.

26. JW, "Translator's Note," *CP*, 90.

27. JW, "Theodor Storm: Foreword," *CP*, 76.

28. From the book jacket for Hermann Hesse, *Wandering*, trans. James Wright and Franz Wright (New York: Farrar, Straus and Giroux, 1972).

29. JW, letter to Helen McNeely Sheriff, June 11, 1972, *AWP*, 375.

30. Hesse, *Wandering*, 7.

31. JW, *Above the River: The Complete Poems* (New York: Farrar, Straus and Giroux and University Press of New England, 1990), xxi.

32. JW, *The Shape of Light* (Buffalo, New York: White Pine Press, 2007), 32–33.

33. JW, "Translator's Note," *CP*, 7.

34. JW, "A Note on Trakl," *CP*, 83.

35. Herbert Lindenberger, letter to Saundra Maley, June 9, 1987.

36. JW, in *1954 Student Workbook*, unpaginated, Theodore Roethke Collection, Special Collections, University of Washington Libraries.

37. JW, in *1954 Student Workbook*, unpaginated.

38. JW, in *1954 Student Workbook*, unpaginated.

39. Herbert Lindenberger, *Georg Trakl* (New York: Twayne, 1971), 65.

40. JW, in *1954 Student Workbook*, unpaginated.

41. JW, in *1954 Student Workbook*, unpaginated.

42. JW, in *1954 Student Workbook*, unpaginated.

43. JW, in *1954 Student Workbook*, unpaginated.

44. Robert Bly, "The Work of James Wright," *PCW*, 78.

45. Bly, "James Wright," *PCW*, 84.

46. Bly, "James Wright," *PCW*, 85.

47. Bly, "James Wright," *PCW*, 97.

48. JW, letter to Robert Bly, July 22, 1958, *AWP*, 112.

49. JW, letter to Robert Bly, *AWP*, 114.

50. JW, letter to Robert Bly, *AWP*, 114.

51. JW, letter to Theodore and Beatrice Roethke, August 5, 1958, *AWP*, 138.

52. JW, "An Interview with Michael Andre," *CP*, 133.

53. Transcription of heavily annotated typescript draft of Trakl's "Lamentation," UMLA.

54. Typescript draft of Trakl's "Grodek," UMLA.

55. JW, "A Note on Trakl," *CP*, 83.

56. John Pilling, *A Reader's Guide to Fifty Modern European Poets* (London: Heinemann; Totowa, NJ: Barnes & Noble, 1982), 167.

Chapter 4: A Fine Weave of Voices: Translation, Whitman, and James Wright's New Style

1. Kevin Stein, *James Wright: Poetry of a Grown Man* (Columbus: Ohio State University Press, 1988), 1–14.

2. JW, letter to Robert Bly, July 23, 1958, *AWP*, 122.

3. JW, letter to Robert Bly, *AWP*, 122.

4. JW, letter to Robert Bly, *AWP*, 123.

5. JW, letter to Robert Bly, *AWP*, 123.

6. Robert Bly and James Wright, "Robert Bly and James Wright: A Correspondence," *Virginia Quarterly Review* 81, no. 1 (2005): 119–20, www.jstor.org /stable/26441729, accessed August 15, 2022.

7. JW, letter to "A Young Writer," February 22, 1959, Upper Midwest Literary Archives, University of Minnesota Libraries, Minneapolis, Minnesota (hereafter cited as UMLA).

8. JW, "The Delicacy of Walt Whitman," *CP*, 5.

9. JW, "The Delicacy," *CP*, 14.

10. JW, "The Delicacy," *CP*, 16.

11. JW, "The Delicacy," *CP*, 19.

12. JW, interview by Peter Stitt, "The Art of Poetry XIX: James Wright," *The Paris Review* 62 (Summer 1975): 58.

13. Here is a selected list from among JW's collected poems of portraits or first-person narratives of persons who are marginalized, unloved, or invisible—"the cheated and the weak," as he characterizes them in "Sparrows in a Hillside Drift":

> From *Saint Judas*: "The Old Man Drunk," "A Note Left in Jimmy Leonard's Shack," "All the Beautiful are Blameless," "American Twilights," "At the Executed Murderer's Grave," "Saint Judas."
>
> From *The Branch Will Not Break*: "A Message Hidden in an Empty Wine Bottle That I Threw into a Gully of Maple Trees One Night at an Indecent Hour," "How My Fever Left," "Miners," "Two Hangovers," "Having Lost My Sons."
>
> From *Shall We Gather at the River*: "In Terror of Hospital Bills," "The Minneapolis Poem," "Inscription for the Tank," "I am a Sioux Brave, He Said in Minneapolis," "The Poor Washed Up by Chicago Winter," "Before a Cashier's Window in a Department Store."
>
> From *New Poems*: "A Centenary Ode: Inscribed to Little Crow, Leader of the Sioux Rebellion in Minnesota, 1862," "Red Jacket's Grave," "Humming a Tune for an Old Lady in West Virginia," "To a Dead Drunk," "Trouble."
>
> From *Two Citizens*: "Ars Poetica: Some Recent Criticism," "Son of

Judas," "The Last Drunk," "Ohio Valley Swains," "The Old WPA Swimming Pool in Martins Ferry, Ohio," "To the Creature of the Creation."

14. *Neruda and Vallejo: Selected Poems*, trans. Robert Bly and James Wright (Boston: Beacon Press, 1971), 213.

15. *Neruda and Vallejo: Selected Poems*, 170. In a brief passage quoted in Bly's introductory notes to Vallejo, Wright is quoted as noting of Vallejo that ". . . he always returns to poems about his family, poems which in their integrity and daring are more beautiful than any other poems on the subject that I have seen."

16. JW, letter to "A Young Writer," April 14, 1959, UMLA.

17. Jonathan Blunk, *James Wright: A Life in Poetry* (New York: Farrar, Straus and Giroux, 2017), 163.

18. Blunk, 164.

19. Peter Ramos, "Beyond the Deep Image: James Wright's Vallejo and the Ethics of Translation," *Mandorla: New Writing from the Americas / Nueva Escritura de las Américas* 9, no. 1 (2006): 254.

20. JW, "Poetry Must Think," an interview with Bruce Henricksen, *CP*, 183.

21. JW, "A Note on Trakl," *CP*, 83.

22. Georg Trakl, *Poems and Prose: A Bilingual Edition*, trans. Alexander Stillmark (Evanston, IL: Northwestern University Press, 2005), xiv.

23. Rainer Maria Rilke, *The Selected Poetry of Rainer Maria Rilke*, trans. Stephen Mitchell (New York: Vintage International, 1998), 61.

24. JW, *CP*, 70. In his "Meditations on René Char," Wright observes: "Rilke's old torso of Apollo warns its beholders that—headless and limbless though it be—there is not one bit of its surface that does not see them, through the skin to the bone and through the bone to the heart. And, says the great Rilke, you cannot bear this vision by staying as you are: 'Du must dein Leben Andern.'"

25. JW, "The Delicacy," *CP*, 4.

26. JW, letter to Michael Cuddihy, September 15, 1979, *AWP*, 543–45.

Chapter 5: Here Is Nourishment: The Spanish Poets

1. JW, letter to Robert Bly, September 4, 1958, *AWP*, 165.

2. JW, letter to Donald Hall, August 14, 1958, *AWP*, 154.

3. JW, letter to Robert Bly, March 1959, UMLA.

4. These excerpts from the poet's journals, notebooks, folders, reproduced images, and unpublished letters are collected in the James Wright papers, Upper Midwest Literary Archives, University of Minnesota Libraries, Minneapolis, Minnesota (hereafter cited as UMLA).

5. Philip Levine, *The Bread of Time* (New York: Alfred A. Knopf, 1994), 159.

6. Edward Thomas, *Cloud Castle and Other Papers* (London: Duckworth, 1922), 101, accessed in books.google.com/books?idHm1bAAAAMAAJ, De-

cember 17, 2023. Here Wright appears to reimagine as poetry these lines from an essay in Thomas's collection entitled "Seven Lamps," even adding his own final couplet.

Chapter 7: Georg Trakl's "Grodek": A Portfolio

1. JW, interview by Peter Stitt, "The Art of Poetry XIX: James Wright," *The Paris Review* 62 (Summer 1975): 49.

2. Robert Bly, Richard Jones, and Kate Daniels, *Of Solitude and Silence: Writings on Robert Bly* (Boston: Beacon Press, 1981), 87.

3. JW, letter to Robert Bly, July 22, 1958, *AWP*, 111.

4. Robert Bly and James Wright, "Robert Bly and James Wright: A Correspondence," *Virginia Quarterly Review* 81, no. 1 (2005): 119–20, www.jstor.org /stable/26441729, accessed August 15, 2022.

5. Bly, Jones, and Daniels, *Of Solitude and Silence*, 89–91.

6. Robert Bly website, www.robertbly.com/r_e_billduffy.html, accessed December 7, 2023.

7. JW, letter to Robert and Carol Bly, September 29, 1959, Robert Bly papers, Upper Midwest Literary Archives, University of Minnesota Libraries, Minneapolis, Minnesota (hereafter cited as UMLA).

8. *Die Dichtungen von Georg Trakl*, Project Gutenberg, www.gutenberg.org /2/9/0/0/29006/, accessed December 7, 2023.

9. *The Penguin Book of German Verse*, ed. and trans. Leonard Wilson Forster (New York: Penguin, 1961), 433.

10. Robert Bly, letter to JW, October 9, 1958, Robert Bly papers, UMLA.

11. Robert Bly, letter to JW, October 9, 1958, Robert Bly papers, UMLA.

12. Figure 7.3, typescript with heavy annotations by Robert Bly and JW, undated, Robert Bly papers, UMLA.

13. Figure 7.7, Bly's handwritten draft with annotations, undated, Robert Bly papers, UMLA.

14. Robert Bly, *The Winged Energy of Delight: Selected Translations* (New York: HarperCollins, 2005), 137.

15. Richard Millington, *The Gentle Apocalypse: Truth and Meaning in the Poetry of Georg Trakl* (Rochester, NY: Boydell and Brewer, 2020), 206–7.

16. Robert Bly, *Winged Energy*, 153.

Afterword

1. JW, letter to Robert Bly, February 14, 1960, Upper Midwest Literary Archives, University of Minnesota Libraries, Minneapolis, Minnesota (UMLA). Wright here quotes Lorca's *Poet in New York*.

2. JW, letter to Dr. Thomas Hodge, June 8, 1979, *AWP*, 536.

Sources for Translations

We have relied largely on source materials we found among the poet's papers now housed in the Upper Midwest Literary Archives at the University of Minnesota. Those materials consisted of loose type-script pages, apparently finished and ready for submission; handwritten drafts among notebook and journal entries; and poems enclosed with letters.

Wherever possible we have followed Wright's dating as it appears on these materials, or as it is alluded to in letters and journal entries. He worked and reworked the translations, as he did his own poems, through many versions—even in a single week. We have hewed as closely in our reconstructions to his purpose as we could, so as to "find some equivalents in your own language, not only equivalents in language itself but equivalents of imagination."

The poems chosen for the Selected Spanish Translations in chapter 3 and the Selected German Translations in chapter 6 represent four groups: 1) full texts of translations and "imitations" discussed and excerpted in *So Much Secret Labor*; 2) published versions of earlier drafts of translations considered in the text; 3) translations published in journals, but uncollected; and 4) translations apparently finished, but never published.

To allow readers to enjoy the Selected Translations as anthologies of poems unencumbered by citation information, we have provided source information here in one place.

Selected Spanish Translations

JUAN RAMÓN JIMÉNEZ

"Skies," February 4 XXXVI, from *Diario de un poeta recién casado* (*Diary of a Newlywed Poet*) 1916. Unpublished draft, dated: January 21, 1959. Upper Midwest Literary Archive (hereafter UMLA).

FEDERICO GARCÍA LORCA

"Air of Night," from *Libro de poemas*, 1921. Unpublished typescript, UMLA.
"Another Dream," from *Libro de poemas*, 1921. Unpublished typescript, UMLA.
"August," from *Canciones*, 1921, first published in *The Sixties*, no. 4 (Fall 1960): 25.
"Dream," from *Libros de poemas*, 1921. Unpublished typescript, UMLA.
"Juan Breve," from *Poema del cante jondo*, 1921, published 1931. Unpublished typescript, dated March 15, 1959, UMLA.
"Lamentations for the Dead." Unpublished typescript, dated March 15, 1959, UMLA.
"Sea," from *Libros de poemas*, 1921. Unpublished typescript, UMLA.
"Afternoon," from *Canciones*,1921–1924, first published in *The Sixties*, no. 4 (Fall 1960). Reprinted in *A Wild Perfection: The Selected Letters of James Wright*, edited by Wright and Maley.

CÉSAR VALLEJO

"I Am Freed from the Burdens of the Sea," from *Trilce* (XLV) 1922, first published in *Chelsea* 7 (May, 1960); first collected in *Twenty Poems of César Vallejo* (1962); reprinted in *Neruda and Vallejo: Selected Poems* (1971 and 1993) and *Collected Poems* (1971).
"Tormented Fugitive, Come In Go Out," from *Trilce* (LIV), 1922, uncollected; first published in *Chelsea* 7 (May, 1960).
"Oh the Four Walls of the Cell," from *Trilce* (XVIII), 1922, uncollected; first published in *Chelsea* 7 (May, 1960).
"At the Border of a Flowering Grave," from *Trilce* (XXIV), 1922, first collected in *Neruda and Vallejo: Selected Poems* (1971 and 1993).
"In that Corner Where We Slept Together," *Trilce* (XV), 1922, first collected in *Neruda and Vallejo: Selected Poems* (1971 and 1993).
"Chalk," from *Los Heraldos Negros*, 1919. Unpublished typescript, UMLA.
"Poem To Be Read and Sung," from *Poemas Humanos*, 1939. Translated by James Wright and Robert Bly. First published in *Crazy Horse* no. 5 (1970); first collected in *Neruda and Vallejo: Selected Poems* (1971 and 1993).
"Have You Anything to Say in Your Defense?" (Espergesia), from *Los Heraldos Negros*, 1919. Published in *Twenty Poems of César Vallejo* (1962); reprinted in *Minnesota Review* 3 (Spring 1963); reprinted in *Neruda and Vallejo: Selected Poems* (1971 and 1993).

"To My Brother Miguel," from *Los Heraldos Negros*, 1919. Translated by John Knoepfle and James Wright. Published in *Twenty Poems of César Vallejo* (1962); reprinted in *Neruda and Vallejo: Selected Poems* (1971 and 1993).

"The Eternal Dice," from *Los Heraldos Negros*, 1919. Published in *Twenty Poems of César Vallejo* (1962); reprinted in *The Sixties* no. 7 (Winter 1964); reprinted in *Neruda and Vallejo: Selected Poems* (1971 and 1993); included in *Collected Poems* (1971); reprinted in *Above the River: The Complete Poems* (1990).

"Our Daily Bread," from *Los Heraldos Negros*, 1919. Published in *Twenty Poems of César Vallejo* (1962); reprinted in Minnesota Review 3 (Spring 1963); reprinted in *Neruda and Vallejo: Selected Poems* (1971 and 1993); included in *Collected Poems* (1971); reprinted in *Above the River: The Complete Poems* (1990).

"What Time Are the Big People Coming Back?," from *Trilce* (III), 1922. First published in *Poetry* no. 98 (September 1961); collected in *Twenty Poems of César Vallejo* (1962); reprinted in *Neruda and Vallejo: Selected Poems* (1971 and 1993); included in *Collected Poems* (1971); reprinted in *Above the River: The Complete Poems* (1990).

"I Stayed Here, Warming the Ink in which I Drown," from *Poemas Humanos*, 1939. Translated by James Wright and Robert Bly. First collected in *Neruda and Vallejo: Selected Poems* (1971 and 1993). See Figure 6.4 for the poem in typescript with handwritten revisions.

"Clapping Palms and Guitars," from *Poemas Humanos*, 1939. Unpublished typescript, UMLA.

"Gunwales of Ice," from *Los Heraldos Negros*, 1919. Unpublished typescript, dated March 3, 1959, UMLA.

"My Accent Trails from My Shoe," from *Poemas Humanos*, 1939. Unpublished typescript, UMLA.

"So Much Hail That I Remember," from *Trilce* (LXXVII), 1922. Translated by Robert Bly and James Wright. First collected in *Neruda and Vallejo: Selected Poems* (1971 and 1993).

PABLO NERUDA

"It Was the Grape's Autumn," from *Canto General*, 1950. Translated by James Wright and Robert Bly. First published *Michigan Quarterly Review* no. 5 (Spring 1966); first collected in *Neruda and Vallejo: Selected Poems* (1971 and 1993).

"They Receive Instructions Against Chile," from *Canto General*, 1950. Translated by James Wright and Robert Bly. First published in *TriQuarterly*, no. 13/14 (Fall 1967); first collected in *Neruda and Vallejo: Selected Poems* (1971 and 1993).

"Friends on the Road (1921)," from *Canto General*, 1950. Translated by James Wright and Robert Bly. First published in *Paris Review* no. 39 (Fall 1966). First collected in *Twenty Poems of Pablo Neruda* (1967); reprinted in *Neruda and Vallejo: Selected Poems* (1971 and 1993). See figures 6.7 and 6.8 for two pages from Wright's notebook, probably from late 1958, discussing his collaboration with Bly on Neruda's "Friends on the Road."

"Ocean," from *Canto General*, 1950. Unpublished, transcribed handwritten draft, UMLA.

JORGE GUILLÉN

"The Snow." This and the next poem, "The Shadows" were enclosed in a letter to Robert and Carol Bly, dated October, 1959.

"The Garden Within," from *Cantico*, 1928–1950. Unpublished typescript. UMLA.

MIGUEL HERNÁNDEZ

"The Train of the Wounded," from *El hombre acecha*, 1939. First published as translated by James Wright with Jaime Calderon, *The Sixties* no. 9 (Spring 1967); first collected in *Miguel Hernández and Blas de Otero: Selected Poems*, edited by Baland and St. Martin (1971).

"War," from *Cancionero y romancero de ausencias*, 1938–1942. First published in *The Sixties* no. 9 (Spring 1967); first collected in *Miguel Hernández and Blas de Otero: Selected Poems*, edited by Baland and St. Martin (1971).

PEDRO SALINAS

"Not in Marble Palaces." Included in *Collected Poems* (1971); reprinted in *Above the River: The Complete Poems* (1990).

Selected German Translations

RAINER MARIA RILKE

"The Water Has Delicate Melodies," from *Erste Gedichte*, 1895. Unpublished draft, UMLA.

"Vigil," an "imitation" of Rilke, from *Erste Gedichte*, 1895. Unpublished draft, UMLA.

"I, 35," from *Das Stundenbuch*, 1905. Unpublished draft. UMLA.

"III, 6," from *Das Stundenbuch*, 1905. Unpublished draft. UMLA.

"Herbst," from *Das Buch der Bilder*, 1902–1906. Unpublished draft. UMLA.

"Orpheus, Eurydike, Hermes," from *Neue Gedichte*, 1907–1908. Published as translated by James Wright and Franz Schneider. *Fresco: The University of Detroit Tri-Quarterly*, n.s., no. 1 (Winter 1961).

"Palm of the Hand," from *Die Gedichte*, 1922–1926. Unpublished draft, UMLA.

"Wenn die Uhren so nah . . . ," from *Die Frühen Gedichte*, 1909. Unpublished draft, UMLA.

HEINRICH HEINE

"Clothes Make the Man: A Song Cycle": Some Imitations of Heinrich
Heine's "*Kleider Machen Lause: ein Liederkranz*," a pastiche of lines from
poems in Heine's *Neue Gedichte*, 1844 and *Buch der Lieder*, 1827. Published in
Kenyon College's literary magazine, *Hika* 17 (Winter 1951).

"Sea Ghost," from *Buch der Lieder*, 1827. Unpublished draft, UMLA. Heine's
last line reads: "Doktor, sind Sie des Teufels?" (Doctor, are you the Devil?).
Among Wright's undergraduate papers there are twenty translations from
Heine, and most of these come from *Buch der Lieder*.

THEODOR STORM

"Woman's Ritornelle." Published in *The Sixties* no. 8 (Spring 1966).

"Orphan." Unpublished typescript, UMLA.

WALTHER VON DER VOGELWEIDE

"Owê war sint verswunden alliu mîniu jâr?" Unpublished typescript, UMLA.

JOHANN WOLFGANG VON GOETHE

"Nature and Art." Unpublished typescript, UMLA. Wright's work contains
more epigraphs from Goethe than from any other poet. Among his papers
there are seven drafts of this translation of "Natur und Kunst," but it was
never published.

EDUARD MÖRIKE

"Soul, Remember," from *Gedichte*, 1876. Unpublished typescript, UMLA.

"Im Frühling," from *Gedichte*, 1876. Translated with Robert Mezey while at
Kenyon College. Unpublished typescript, UMLA.

HERMANN HESSE

"Lonely Evening," from *Der Blütenzweig: Eine Auswahl aus den Gedichten von
Hermann Hesse*, 1945. Unpublished typescript, UMLA.

"Brother Death," from *Der Blütenzweig: Eine Auswahl aus den Gedichten von
Hermann Hesse*, 1945. Unpublished typescript, UMLA.

"In Fog," from *Der Blütenzweig: Eine Auswahl aus den Gedichten von Hermann
Hesse*, 1945. Unpublished typescript, UMLA.

These three Hesse translations made at Kenyon College were not among
those published in 1970 in Wright's translation of Hesse's *Poems*.

GEORG TRAKL

"Transfiguration," from *Siebengesang des Todes*, 1913–1914. Unpublished type-
script, UMLA.

"The Wanderer," from *Siebengesang des Todes*, 1913–1914. Unpublished type-
script, UMLA.

"The Return Home," from *Poems der Brenner*, 1914–1915. Unpublished typescript, UMLA.

"Amen," from *Gedichte*, 1913. Unpublished typescript, UMLA.

JOSEPH VON EICHENDORFF

"Joy of Death," an "imitation" from *Gedichte von Joseph von Freiherrn Eichendorff*, 1837. Unpublished typescript, UMLA.

NIKOLAUS LENAU

"Loneliness," an "adaptation from the German of Nicolas Lenau." Unpublished typescript, UMLA. Lenau was one of the first Germans translated by Wright at Kenyon College, and he speaks of this poet in a short story called "The Germans," which he also wrote at Kenyon.

James Wright as Translator: A Selected Bibliography

I. Individual and Edited Volumes of Translations (in order of publication date)

Char, Renè. *Hypnos Waking*. Translated by Jackson Matthews with Barbara Howes, W. S. Merwin, William Jay Smith, Richard Wilbur, William Carlos Williams, and James Wright. New York: Random House, 1956.

Flores, Angel, ed. *An Anthology of Spanish Poetry from Garcilaso to García Lorca*. Garden City, NY: Doubleday & Co. Inc., 1961.

Trakl, Georg. *Twenty Poems of Georg Trakl*. Translated and selected by James Wright and Robert Bly. Madison, MN: Sixties Press, 1961.

Vallejo, César. *Twenty Poems of César Vallejo*. Translated by James Wright, Robert Bly, and John Knoepfle. Madison, MN: Sixties Press, 1963.

Storm, Theodor. *The Rider on the White Horse*. Translated by James Wright. New York: Signet Books, 1964.

Guillén, Jorge. Cántico: Selection. Edited by Norman Thomas DiGiovanni. Boston: Little, Brown and Company, 1965.

Neruda, Pablo. *Twenty Poems of Pablo Neruda*. Translated by James Wright and Robert Bly. Madison, MN: Sixties Press, 1967.

Rothenberg, Jerome, ed. *Technicians of the Sacred: A Range of Poetries from Africa, America, Asia, Europe, and Oceania*. Garden City, NY: Doubleday & Co., 1969.

Hesse, Hermann. *Poems*. Translated by James Wright. New York: Farrar, Straus and Giroux, 1970.

Neruda, Pablo, and César Vallejo. *Selected Poems*. Translated by Robert Bly and James Wright. Boston: Beacon Press, 1971.

Wright, James. *Collected Poems*. Middletown, CT: Wesleyan University Press, 1971.

Hesse, Hermann. *Wandering*. Translated by James Wright and Franz Wright. New York: Farrar, Straus and Giroux, 1972.

Hernández, Miguel, and Blas de Otero. *Selected Poems*. Edited by Timothy
   Baland and Hardie St. Martin. Translated by Timothy Baland, Robert
   Bly, Hardie St. Martin, and James Wright. Boston: Beacon Press, 1972.
Graziano, Frank, ed. *Georg Trakl: A Profile*. Durango, CO: Logbridge-
   Rhodes, 1983.
Jiménez, Juan Ramón. *Light and Shadows: Selected Poems and Prose*. Edited
   by Dennis Maloney. Translated by Robert Bly, Dennis Maloney, Antonio
   T. de Nicholas, James Wright, and Clark Zlotchew. Fredonia, NY: White
   Pine Press, 1987.
Wright, James. *Above the River: The Complete Poems. A Wesleyan University
   Press Edition*. New York: Farrar, Straus, and Giroux and University Press
   of New England, 1990.

II. Additional Books by James Wright with Considerable Relevance to His Translations

Wright, James. *Collected Prose*. Edited by Anne Wright. Ann Arbor: Univer-
   sity of Michigan Press, 1982. [Important source of essays on translating:
   Char; Storm; Vallejo; Trakl; and Hesse, a review of Nathaniel Tarn's trans-
   lation of Neruda's *The Heights of Macchu Picchu*, as well as several interviews
   in which translations and translating are discussed.]
Wright, James. *A Wild Perfection: The Selected Letters of James Wright*. Edited
   by Anne Wright and Saundra Rose Maley. New York: Farrar, Straus and
   Giroux, 2005. [Contains many letters on translating Trakl, Vallejo, Rilke,
   Neruda, Lorca, and Char; along with dozens of letters to Robert Bly on
   the subject, and a rich appendix of poems including several unpublished
   translations.]

III. Critical Sources Related to Wright's Translations

Blunk, Jonathan. *James Wright: A Life in Poetry*. New York: Farrar, Straus and
   Giroux, 2017. [An excellent source for discussions of translating poetry in
   general, and specifically on: Neruda, Vallejo, Rilke, Trakl, and working
   with Robert Bly.]
Gustafson, Mark. *Born Under the Sign of Odin: The Life and Times of Robert
   Bly's Little Magazine and Small Press*. Minneapolis, MN: Nodin House,
   2021.
Maley, Saundra Rose. *Solitary Apprenticeship: James Wright and German Po-
   etry*. Lewiston, NY: Mellen University Press, 1996. [Most comprehensive
   source of information on Wright's translations from the German poets,
   from the mid-nineteenth century to Trakl. Includes nearly 200 pages of
   his translations gathered from the Wright papers now housed at the Upper
   Midwest Literary Archives, University of Minnesota.]

IV. Additional Sources Consulted

Adler, Jeremy. "You Dying Nations." *The London Review of Books* 25, no. 8 (2003). www.lrb.co.uk/the-paper/v25/no8/jeremy-adler/you-dying-nations.

Benjamin, Walter. "The Task of the Translator." In *Illuminations*, edited by Hannah Arendt, 69–82. New York: Schocken Books, 1978.

Bly, Robert, Richard Jones, and Kate Daniels. *Of Solitude and Silence: Writings on Robert Bly*. Boston: Beacon Press, 1981.

Bly, Robert. "The Eight Stages of Translation." *The Kenyon Review* 4, no. 2 (1982): 68–89. www.jstor.org/stable/43352701.

Bly, Robert, and James Wright. "Robert Bly and James Wright: A Correspondence." *The Virginia Quarterly Review* 81, no. 1 (2005): 104–31. www.jstor.org/stable/26441729.

Breslin, James E. B. *From Modern to Contemporary American Poetry, 1945–1965*. Chicago: University of Chicago Press, 1983.

Copeland, Todd William. "A James Wright Research Guide: Bibliography of Primary Works, Bibliography of Secondary Works, and Other Reference Material in English." PhD diss., Texas A&M University, 2000.

Doctorow, E. L. "James Wright at Kenyon." *Gettysburg Review* 3, no. 2 (Winter 1990): 11–22.

Elkins, Andrew. *The Poetry of James Wright*. Tuscaloosa: University of Alabama Press, 1991.

Firmage, Robert. *Song of the West: Selected Poems of Georg Trakl*. San Francisco, CA: North Point Press, 1988.

Forster, Leonard Wilson, ed. *The Penguin Book of German Verse*. Translated by Leonard Wilson Forster. New York: Penguin, 1959.

Gass, William H. *Reading Rilke: Reflecting on the Problems of Translation*. Champaign, IL: Dalkey Archive Press, 2015.

Gattuccio, Nicholas. "Now My Amenities of Stone Are Done: Some Notes on the Style of James Wright." *Scape* no. 1 (1981): 31–44.

Gustafson, Mark. "Bringing Blood to Trakl's Ghost." *Antioch Review* 72, no. 4 (2014): 636–54.

Heine, Heinrich. *Selected Verse*. Translated by Peter Branscombe. Harmondsworth and New York: Penguin, 1986.

Hugo, Richard. *The Triggering Town*. New York: W. W. Norton, 1979.

Kalaidjian, Walter. "Many of Our Waters: The Poetry of James Wright." *boundary 2* 9, no. 2 A Supplement on Contemporary Poetry (Winter 1981): 101–21.

Kirsch, Adam. "Primal Ear." *The New Yorker* (August 8, 2005). newyorker.com/magazine/2005/08/08/primal-ear.

Lensing, George S., and Ronald Moran. *Four Poets and the Emotive Imagination: Bly, Wright, Simpson and Stafford*. Baton Rouge: Louisiana State University Press, 1976.

Levine, Philip. *The Bread of Time*. New York: Alfred A. Knopf, 1994.

Lindenberger, Herbert. *Georg Trakl*. New York: Twayne, 1971.

Louth, Charlie. "Early Poems." In *The Cambridge Companion to Rilke*, edited by Karen Leeder and Robert Vilain, 41–58. Cambridge: Cambridge University Press, 2010.

Mazzaro, Jerome. "Dark Water: James Wright's Early Poetry." *Centennial Review* 27, no. 2 (1983): 135–55.

Millington, Richard. *The Gentle Apocalypse: Truth and Meaning in the Poetry of Georg Trakl*. Rochester, NY: Boydell and Brewer, 2020.

Murdoch, Brian O. "Translation and Dissection: Teaching the Modern German Lyric: Rilke's 'Herbsttag' and Trakl's 'Grodek.'" *Die Unterrichtpraxis/ Teaching German* 13, no. 1 (Spring 1980): 13–21. www.jstor.org/stable/3530821.

Orlen, Steve. "The Green Wall." *Ironwood* 10 (1977).

Phillips, Rodney. *The Hand of the Poet: Poems and Papers in Manuscript*. New York: Rizzoli, 1997.

Pilling, John. *A Reader's Guide to Fifty Modern European Poets*. London: Heinemann; Totowa, NJ: Barnes and Noble, 1982.

Prawer, S. S., ed. *The Penguin Book of Lieder*. Translated by S. S. Prawer. London: Penguin, 1996.

Ramos, Peter. "Beyond the Deep Image: James Wright's Vallejo and the Ethics of Translation,"
Mandorla: New Writing from the Americas/ Nueva Escritura de las Americas 9, no. 1 (2006): 236–61.

Rilke, Rainer Maria. *The Poetry of Rilke: Bilingual Edition*. Translated by Edward Snow. New York: North Point Press, 2009.

———. *Selected Poems*. Translated by Robert Bly. New York: Harper Perennial, 1981.

———. *The Selected Poetry of Rainer Maria Rilke*. Translated by Stephen Mitchell. New York: Vintage International, 1998.

———. *The Book of Hours: A New Translation with Commentary*. Translated by Susan Ranson. Rochester, NY: Camden House, 2012.

Roberson, William H. *James Wright: An Annotated Bibliography*. Lanham, MD: Scarecrow Press, 1995.

Simpson, Louis. *Ships Going into the Blue*. Ann Arbor: University of Michigan Press, 1994.

Smith, Dave, ed. *The Pure Clear Word: Essays on the Poetry of James Wright*. Urbana: University of Illinois Press, 1982.

Stein, Kevin. *James Wright: Poetry of a Grown Man*. Columbus: Ohio State University Press, 1988.

Stitt, Peter. "The Art of Poetry XIX: James Wright." *The Paris Review* 62 (Summer 1975): 34–61.

Trakl, Georg. *Poems and Prose: A Bilingual Edition*. Translated by Alexander Stillmark. Evanston, IL: Northwestern University Press, 2005.

Vallejo, César. *Selected Writings of César Vallejo*. Translated by Joseph W. Mulligan. Middletown, CT: Wesleyan University Press, 2015.

Waters, William. "The New Poems." In *The Cambridge Companion to Rilke*, edited by Karen Leeder and Robert Vilain, 59–73. Cambridge: Cambridge University Press, 2010.

Wright, James. In "James Wright: A Special Issue," *Ironwood* 10 (1977).

———. "A Complaint for George Doty in the Death House." *The Paris Review* 9 (Summer 1955).

———. "Elegiac Verses for Theodor Storm." *Hika* 16 (Summer 1951). digital. kenyon.edu/hika/73.

———. "Kleider machen Lause ein Liederkranz (Clothes Make the Man: A Song Cycle): Some Imitations of Heinrich Heine's German." *Hika* 17 (Winter 1951). digital.kenyon.edu/hika/71.

———. "The Quest," *The New Yorker* 30 (October 1954).

———. "To A Visitor from My Hometown (an Imitation of Walter von der Vogelweide)." *Assay* 14 (Winter/Spring 1957).

———. "Vision and Elegy." *Hika* 15 (Fall 1950). digital.kenyon.edu/hika/87.

Yatchisin, George. "A Listening to Walt Whitman and James Wright." *Walt Whitman Quarterly Review* 9, no. 4 (1992): 175–95.

V. Manuscript Collections

James Wright. Papers. Upper Midwest Literary Archives. University of Minnesota Library.

Robert Bly. Papers. Upper Midwest Literary Archives. University of Minnesota Library.

Index

About the Authors

ANNE WRIGHT was born in New York City and grew up in Greenwich, Connecticut. After graduating from Wheelock College in 1950 she taught for forty-two years, working with students of varied ages, from nursery school to young adults. She met and married James Wright in 1967 in New York City, which became their home. The couple collaborated on a book of prose pieces, *The Summers of Annie and James Wright: Sketches and Mosaics* (1981). After James's death in 1980, she edited five of his books: *This Journey* (1982), *Collected Prose* (1983), *The Secret Field: Selections from the Final Journals of James Wright* (1985), *Above the River: The Complete Poems* (1992), and *The Delicacy and Strength of Lace: Letters Between Leslie Marmon Silko and James Wright* (2009). She also co-edited, alongside Saundra Rose Maley, a book of letters, *A Wild Perfection: The Selected Letters of James Wright* (2005).

SAUNDRA ROSE MALEY co-edited *A Wild Perfection: The Selected Letters of James Wright* with Anne Wright (2005). She is the author of the poetry collection *Disappearing Act* (2015) and the scholarly work *Solitary Apprenticeship: James Wright and German Poetry* (1996), and co-author of *The Art of the Footnote* (1996) and *The Research Guide for the Digital Age* (1997) with Francis Burkle-Young.

JEFF KATZ is the former vice president of information services, dean of libraries, and executive director of the Hannah Arendt Center for

Politics and Humanities at Bard College in Annandale-on-Hudson, New York. He has written two books of poetry, *Mythos* (2019) and *Small Rain* (2004), and he co-edited *Thinking in Dark Times: Hannah Arendt on Ethics and Politics* (2010). He lives with his wife in the Hudson Valley.